Progress Leadership
Say NO to Change Management

Dean Lindsay
Progress Agent

Ashini,
Be Progress,
Dean

Progress
Leadership
Say NO to
Change
Management

Dean Lindsay
Progress Agent

INFORMATION IS YUMMY
WORLD GUMBO
PUBLISHING

WWW.WORLDGUMBO.COM

First Edition 2021

ISBN-13: 978-0-9761141-7-8

Progress Agent®, Progress Leadership® and Big PHAT Goals®
are Registered Trademarks of Dean Lindsay
and The Progress Agents LLC.

ATTENTION CORPORATIONS, UNIVERSITIES, COLLEGES, AND PROFESSIONAL ORGANIZATIONS:

Quantity discounts are available on bulk purchases of this book for
educational, gift purposes, or as premiums for increasing magazine
subscriptions or renewals. Special books or book excerpts can
also be created to fit specific needs. **For more information,
please contact: 214-457-5656**

Cover Design by *Jose Cordova*

To Ella, Sofia and Lena

Contents

Foreword by Julie Weber,
Vice President and Chief People Officer,
Southwest Airlines

First thing's first: *Progress Leadership: Say No to Change Management* is a great book arriving at the perfect time. It is fun to read and crammed full of thought-provoking, practical and motivating take-aways. I recommend this book to HR Professionals, business leaders, sales leaders, and anyone who is trying to not only navigate the business world today, but also to succeed in it. With the 6 Ps of Progress, Dean gives all of us the incredible opportunity to be purposeful in creating progress—not just change—in our lives and work.

If only I had read this book prior to the Tech Bubble burst in 2001! While working at a software company, like many of my fellow HR Professionals, I was doing my best to "lead change," to "manage change," in an unprecedented time when high technology companies dramatically went from such incredible highs on Wall Street to such devastating lows in a short period of time. We were reeling from the emotional shock and uncertainty after the events of 9/11. This book would have provided a new way of looking at change management, and also a more hopeful way of beginning to answer the question "what now?".

Thankfully, now I have insight from this book, because over the past year, I've faced the worst crisis of my career. I'd venture to guess many of us have. So, here we are again in the midst of unprecedented times. In fact, the word "unprecedented" was arguably one of the most-used words of 2020.

The year was unprecedented for all of us as human beings. It was unprecedented for our society. It was unprecedented for businesses. And it was most definitely unprecedented for business leaders who suddenly found themselves creating infectious disease policies, managing remote workforces, and, often, trying to save their companies in the face of breathtaking financial decline. How do you protect your organization while also protecting jobs and pay for every employee? How do you ensure a diverse, equitable, and inclusive workforce? Those are just two examples of the questions that kept many a leader up at night.

So, what now? As we emerge from a global pandemic and civic unrest, HR Professionals face a tough labor market—job openings have increased while job applications have decreased, so there are fewer candidates for more positions.

When it comes to existing workforces, leaders face the decision of whether to return remote employees to the office and how to maintain a strong culture if they decide to remain remote. They wrestle with how to navigate racial and gendered inequities in our society, and carefully consider how diversity, equity, and inclusion should be navigated in the workplace.

Oh, and they're pondering these massive questions while still trying to recover from (in many cases) a devastating financial year. (During Southwest's worst week in 2020, our traffic was down 97 percent. For the first time in 47 years, we did not make a profit.)

Now, more than ever, Progress Leadership is a must read for all of us. Only the businesses that are able to grow, gain market share, win new customers, and build upon employee loyalty and engagement while attracting top candidates will survive. That requires more than change management; it requires progress. It requires committing to progress. And, it requires persistence.

I am so fortunate to be working for Southwest Airlines, especially as we celebrate a momentous occasion— our 50th anniversary. Uniforms have changed. Technology has changed. What hasn't changed is our belief that taking care of our Employees and Customers is critical to our success. (For starters, the "C" in Customers and the "E" in Employees are capitalized deliberately).

In describing the 6 Ps of Progress (I won't give away too much!), Dean captures why Southwest Airlines Employees provide such incredible Customer Service. We love what we do and our Company loves us! We have a promise to Employees: Employees will be provided the same concern, respect, and caring attitude within the organization that they are expected to share externally with every Southwest Customer. It seems only fair, right? And, we work unusually hard during the selection process to hire Employees who have a natural desire to serve others.

We hire for attitude and train for skill. (Don't worry—we still hire incredibly skilled Pilots!) Yeah, some skills are hard to train, but it's impossible to train someone to have a great attitude and to enjoy their work, their Customers, and their fellow Employees.

Our values are segmented as "Me" (How I Show Up), "We" (How We Treat Each Other), and "Southwest" (How Southwest Succeeds). They're described in easy-to-understand ways; for example: Don't make the easy hard. Act like an owner. Live by The Golden Rule. Don't be rude. Don't be a jerk. These values outline how we conduct ourselves, how we interact with one another and our Customers, and how we will succeed—together. Having personal values that align with Southwest values is more important than any skill.

There will be a next "unprecedented" time. What Dean explains in a witty and entertaining way is that our attitudes, our ability to endure and successfully emerge over and over, and our chance to get what we want out of this life, is up to each one of us. I have always believed "if it is meant to be, it is up to me." Dean explains why that rings true, and provides the tools make it happen! We have to grab every minute of every day and create progress in our work and lives. We own it. I own it. I will be progress.

You've done it again! This book is so timely, Dean. Thank you.

— Julie Weber,
Vice President and Chief People Officer,
Southwest Airlines

Committing to Progress Leadership

"A human being is a deciding being."
— *Dr. Viktor Frankl*

Commit to Progress Leadership ®
Say NO to Change Management!

The business term *"change management"* has been around for a good long while. The term relates to *"initiating significant change"* within an organization's processes. This change can include anything from altering organizational culture to embracing diversity to modifying an individual's work tasks to increasing morale and loyalty to an organization's mission & vision.

The goal behind *"initiating significant change"* may be solid, but the problem with the term "change management" along with the focus on "change management" is that no one actually desires or plans to change. We desire and plan to *progress*. **Change is inevitable, progress is a choice. All progress is change, but not all change is progress.**

We do not want managers to manage our change. **We want leaders to lead our progress.** Let's focus on what *"initiating significant change"* truly should be: *Progress Leadership.* Leaders should position challenges as opportunities for advancement and not merely problems to be solved to get us back to where we were. As Albert Einstein said, *"In the middle of difficulty lies opportunity."*

In a time of continual transformation, committed leaders should focus on inspiring and influencing progress, not supervising change. As leaders, we must be viewed as catalysts in their progress, agents in their progress. We must be viewed as **Progress Agents** not merely change agents.

15

We – along with our leadership, organizations, solutions, directions, guidance, vision, strategy, communication style, our organization's mission & vision, products, and services – must be positioned <u>AS</u> *progress* in the minds of those we intend to lead and inspire to positive action. **We must Be Progress in their minds.**

> **"If you want to build a ship, don't drum up people together to collect wood and don't assign them tasks and work, but rather teach them to long for the endless immensity of the sea."**
> — *Antoine de Saint-Exupéry*

It is <u>reasons</u> that shape, nourish, and sustain the thoughts that create the actions necessary to reach desired results. Organizations are most successful at *"initiating significant change"* when the <u>reasons to act</u> connect personally with the individual employees making the alteration in behavior. **If the reasons don't connect with the individual, then the *planned progress* will be viewed as merely change and will be resisted or at least not acted on.** Team members may still be physically clock in but have mentally checked out.

Progress Agents don't just TELL people what to do, we include others in the *progress* as well as the *process and* work to positively influence thoughts and feelings by sharing reasons to act.

> **"The key to successful leadership is influence, not authority."**
> — *Ken Blanchard*

We live in a world of influence. We are influenced to purchase this, to believe that, to participate in this activity, to attend that event. This is not a bad thing. Most often it is good. Our parents influenced our decision not to play with fire. Our best friend influenced our decision not to wear corduroy.

> **"There is only one way... to get anybody to do anything. And that is by making the other person want to do it."**
> — *Dale Carnegie*

Dale Carnegie wrote his classic *How to Win Friends and Influence People* way back in 1936, and its wisdom is no less true and vibrantly powerful today. The book is packed with insight on leading and building strong relationships by lifting people up, making them feel good, and "spurring people on to success."

Wisely, the book is not called *How to Lift People Up and Make Them Feel Good* or *How to Spur People on to Success.* No, Carnegie's classic is appropriately titled: *How to <u>Win</u> Friends and <u>Influence</u> People. And who is doing the winning?* It's you and me, along with the person being lifted up, made to feel good, and spurred on to success (*read: influenced and led*).

In his book, Mr. Carnegie encourages us to, among other things: *Talk in terms of the other person's interests, respect others' opinions, try honestly to see things from the other person's point of view, and try to make the other person happy about doing the things you suggest.* In other words, genuinely care about people and their feelings.

17

But Mr. Carnegie's classic does not only encourage us to take these actions for the benefit of the people we are respecting and "making happy."

The book doesn't even make the argument that it is even morally right to care about people's feelings *(although I am sure Mr. Carnegie would agree that it is).* No, the book simply makes the clear case that caring about others' feelings is good for the person (or organization) who cares.

Intense focus on feelings in a time of transformation is often described as the *"human side of change management."* This always gives me pause.

The "human side" of business—what other side is there?

Some might say the organization's side. *So then, the organization and the humans are on different sides?*

That's the problem right there. Organizations are formed by people (humans) partnering to get their wants and needs met by helping other people (humans) get their wants and needs met.

> **"Humanize globalization and globalize humanization."**
> — *Father Anselm Gruen*

Leaders who do not take the individual into account and do not plan for the human side of *Progress* often find themselves scratching their heads about where their plans went wrong. You develop a fuzzy point of view when all you focus on is you.

Let me be very clear, it takes more than the title of supervisor, manager, or "change agent" to lead people in the direction of progress.

We all want to be in relationships with people, as well as partner with organizations that bring progress to our lives. Without personal commitment to execute, new organizational plans and initiatives often fail. Execution is assured by establishing clear links between goals, motivations, strategy, and team members.

> **"Management is about arranging and telling. Leadership is about nurturing and enhancing."**
> —*Tom Peters*

Make no mistake about it, *all leadership begins with self.* Committing to Progress Leadership means personally striving to help others find meaning in their work. Committing to Progress leadership means working to understand and communicate how a team member's personal goals can dovetail with the organization's goals and thus create true commitment that gets the team member to act – because he or she wants to, not because they have to.

Leaders committed to being progress in an ever-changing world *(Progress Agents)* focus on helping all progress not on making some comply. **Progress Agents** thus create an organizational culture in which empowered employees are committed to finding what is *truly* the next step forward. Also, just because an organization is getting bigger does not mean it is progressing. A serious challenge for companies large and small is to progress, and not just change.

Committing to Progress Leadership enhances employee engagement and morale because moving our focus from change management to progress leadership creates a shift in power from wielding power over employees to creating power among employees. Progress Leadership helps all team members create the internal drive needed to focus on and commit to an organization's mission and vision.

"You manage things; you lead people."
— *Rear Admiral Grace Murray Hopper*

Our ability to lead personal and professional progress is directly related to how successful we are at helping others progress. This book offers a fresh and powerful blueprint for leading progress in this complicated, stress-inducing, world of radical change. Its transferable concepts are offered to help inspire progress-based action within yourself and others, and reap the bounty of higher (and happier) performance levels in your organizations.

There should be some ideas, tips, and strategies in this book that make you think, *"I knew that. That's common sense."* Beware of anything that, after some thought, does NOT seem like common sense. The unfortunate truth about common sense is that it's rarely common practice. The tough journey, in leadership and in life, is to travel the long road from "always KNEW" to "always DO."

In these pages, you'll learn how to help yourself and your team enhance opportunities by implementing and using what I call the *Six Ps of Progress* which I will introduce and discuss in detail in this book.

20

However, simply learning <u>how</u> to enhance opportunities by being aware of the Six Ps is not the goal. The goal is to <u>actually enhance</u> your opportunities and those of your team by <u>using</u> the Six Ps of Progress in your life and work. **Execution is vital.** Learning should not lead to simply knowing. Learning should lead to <u>action</u>. True Progress Leadership requires well-planned, progress-based action.

My aim is for you to USE these concepts to create strong resolve that ignites and sustains progress toward team goals, even as the world continues to shift and creak around us. Leading progress in this ever-changing world in turn creates better leaders, better team members, better human beings. Leading progress for ourselves and others establishes and cements customer loyalty, generates quality referrals, and leads to career development and job satisfaction.

There is a powerful and important connection between solid leadership, sales success, true customer loyalty and organizational culture improvements. All are achieved by effectively positioning ideas, recommendations, solutions, products, services – even ourselves – as progress in the minds of those we intend to lead or to inspire to positive action.

The key is to focus on being Progress not merely making progress. Committed leaders progress as they help others progress. **Committed leaders are Progress Agents NOT *Change Agents.***

Commit to Progress Leadership. Say NO to Change Management. Be a Progress Agent. *Be Progress.*

Super Quick Action Steps to Excel at Progress Leadership

Commit to Leading Progress in an Ever-changing World.
Be Passionate About Your Work.
Be Passionate About Your Team.
Be Passionate About Your LIFE.
Internalize, but Do Not Personalize.
- work to not take stuff too personally, even when someone means it personally.
Be Human. Be Humane.
Accentuate the Progress.
Compliment with Reason.
Smile with Reason.
Get Enough Sleep.
Read Good Stuff.
Be Patient.
Exercise.
Share Your Expertise.
Eat a Healthy Breakfast.
Look Sharp. Feel Sharp.
Drink Water. Drink More Water.
Maximize Your Personal Potential.
Get a Massage. Get Another Massage.
Care and Listen. Care and Listen Some More.
Get to Know Others' Parameters for Progress.
Surround Yourself with Self-Motivating Experts.
Cherish & Cultivate Constructive Communication.
Craft Big PHAT Personal & Organizational Goals.
Ask Questions that Show Respect and Value.

Be Progress.

Detailed action steps for excelling at Progress Leadership in the **To Thy Progress Agent Self Be True** *section of this book.*

To Change Is Human; to Progress, Divine.

Every day, every hour, every minute, we're changing and so is our world. Some may feel resistant to change, and even claim to be personally unchangeable, yet the presence of change is one of the few constants. Marriage, graduation, a new job, the birth of a child: all bring change. But so do eating a big lunch, seeing a sad movie, and meeting someone new. We experience and relate to change daily. Every day we have a slightly new normal.

Change happens. We can't avoid change. We are always in some form of transition, always arriving at some new *place* and dealing with new rollouts, new ideas, new everything. The very molecules inside the cells of our bodies are in constant flux.

Significant change can arrive like an Oklahoma twister, picking us up, shaking our sense of identity, and then dropping us way outside of our comfort zone.
The ailing economy and the tough business climate *(not to mention the real climate and global pandemics)* make it easy to understand why so many people have trouble finding ways to get and stay moving toward progress. It may feel like a safe place, but it is dangerous to live in denial.

Our world and our lives are always changing, but they are not always progressing. Yet, opportunities for progress still exist, even in the most challenging of times. It is natural to resist what we view as change. However, we embrace what we view as progress.

Progress means: forward movement, advance, gradual betterment. It takes awareness, character, discipline, and effort to progress.

The word *progress* carries a forward thrust and focus, a vibrant and transcendent quality that the words *change* and even *success* don't deliver. With every *success* comes the desire for more success.

When we reach a goal, our natural ambitiousness tells us that the goal is also the stepping stone to the next, possibly more rewarding and worthwhile, goal. Therefore, every success establishes a *new norm,* and brings with it the question: *What next*?

"Don't aim at success. The more you aim at it and make it a target, the more you are going to miss it."
— *Dr. Viktor Frankl*

The road to success is always under construction. We are always striving for something. (I will share that the something I am referring to is not a person, place, or thing, but rather a feeling. A mixture of six feelings, to be exact, but we will deal with that soon enough.) Continual striving can become quite unpleasant and unhealthy if we do not take time to soak in the positive buzz – feelings – from our forward momentum.

When we focus on leading daily progress, for ourselves and others, we are able to feel daily satisfaction. With every forward step, we see more clearly, our confidence grows, our position improves, and our options multiply. We progress toward today's goal on the strength of our past progress. Once achieved, today's goal becomes tomorrow's launching pad.

When a new opportunity comes our way, we each internalize it, and size it up as Progress or Change. This new opportunity could be starting a new business relationship, working extra hours on a project, getting up to speed on a new product line, working to meet quota, anything. Again, **all progress is change, but not all change is progress.**

Let's say I have an upset stomach. *"Man, I've got a stomachache. Ouch! My stomach is killing me. This has got to change."* Somebody hears me, walks over, and punches me in the nose. *Is that change?* Yeah, it's change. But it's not progress. Well, maybe to the person who punched me, but not to me.

What may seem like progress (good) to one person or group of people may seem like change (bad) to another. Propaganda, book burning, even war and murder are all thought of as "progress" at some point in the minds of the perpetrators (scary). Because progress is subjective, there is no single factor that clearly determines whether an event represents progress or change.

However, we can say that we:

- **Start businesses** *to progress, not change*
- **Work on teams** *to progress, not change*
- **Make the tough choices and the tough phone calls** *to progress, not change*
- **Join an organization** *to progress, not change*
- **Spend our hard-earned money** *to progress, not change. (We would rather keep our change than change, but will offer our best to progress.)*

25

As we age, we realize that slowing change can be progress. Think of the fifty-year-old swimmer who manages to equal her performance from five years before. Maintenance is progress in that it avoids change for the worse.

We do not want life-changing products, services, experiences, ideas, and opportunities. We want life-progressing products, services, experiences, ideas and opportunities.

We live in a "next big thing" world. As leaders, we should be careful not to mistake different for progress. Just because something is new or flashy does not mean it is right or adds meaning to our work or lives. However, because all progress is change, people who claim to be 100% resistant to ANY change are often choosing to be resistant to the possibility of progress.

Progress does not demand perfection, only persistence.

To Change Is Human; to Progress, Divine.
Be Progress.

Quick shout out to Alex Pope:
If he were among us today, eighteenth-century English poet Alexander Pope would likely be one popular guy on social media. It was he who wrote the lofty words, "To err is human; to forgive, divine." Pope is said to be the third most frequently quoted writer in the English language, after Shakespeare and Tennyson. *Alexander may not be on social media or the internet, but I am, and would be happy to get connected with you:*

YouTube: DeanLindsay   Twitter: @DeanLindsay
LinkedIn: @Dean Lindsay   Instagram: @DeanoLindsay
Facebook: @DeanLindsayProgressAgent

Internalized Reasons
Create Movement
Motivated to Lead Progress?

I read a funny cartoon in *Fast Company* magazine a good while back. It was of two fish swimming next to each other. One of the fish had a hook dangling from its mouth. That fish said, *"Oh, it was a scary couple of minutes, but now I am making a fortune as a motivational speaker."*

Several times over the years I have been referred to as a *Motivational Speaker* and at first, I really didn't care for it. I had this image of a *Motivational Speaker* as being a kind of smarmy, slightly plastic and over-the-top *"people person,"* who sprinted through crowds giving everybody high fives, before ascending to the podium to share his rags-to-riches-to-rags-to-riches story. He or she might then encourage seminar goers to turn to their neighbor and repeat a soulful mantra like, *"I am. I will. I can,"* followed by a cleansing breath, a mindful hokey pokey, the sharing of a deep secret and a good cathartic cry.

But as I sought the <u>fundamental meaning</u> of being motivational, I came to realize that each of us has the need and the opportunity to be motivational every day of our lives.
- Committed leaders are motivational
- Committed team members are motivational
- Committed professionals are motivational
- Committed customer-service representatives are motivational
- Committed sales professionals are motivational

27

I sure as heck better be motivational. As a leader, you better be, too. *Why else would others listen to us or be led by us?*

We each may be motivational, but the decision to <u>be</u> motivated is a personal choice. I can't motivate you and you can't motivate me. I may be motivational. You may be motivational. But truly, no one IS a motivator. The only person who can actually motivate you is you.

> **"Motivation is a fire from within.**
> **If someone else tries to light that fire under you,**
> **chances are it will burn very briefly."**
> — *Stephen Covey*

The word motivation can be broken down into two root words: Motive and Action.

Motive is an inner drive that prompts a person to *act* in a certain way. Motive is the goal or object of one's action. Other words for motive include reasons, purpose, intention.

Action is simply the doing of something. *Examples of actions include:* Do, smile, listen, read, act, try, sign up, show up, eat, move.

Motivation, therefore, is the *inner drive to act, to do, to try.*

Simply put:
Internalized Reasons Create Movement.

As William Shakespeare wrote in *The Life and Death of King John*, *"Strong reasons make strong actions."* Often, we fixate on a goal without giving enough focus and attention to the reasons behind the goal. **It is not a goal that motivates us, but our internalized reasons behind the goal that propel us to action.**

Many of us do not need to come to terms with the world around us. Instead, we need to come to terms with our own unrealistic expectations and poorly defined goals. As we connect with the fact that our internal reasons inspire our external actions, we begin to notice that our true enemies come from within. Among these resident vixens:

- Self-doubt
- Stress & Anxiety
- Impatience & Procrastination
- Lack of focus
- Poor self-management (time management)
- Misguided pursuit of perfection
- Fear of success

As leaders, the most important things we can help our team members carry with them are their strong reasons why. Well-established reasons help us feel the internal pressure needed to focus. We must dig to the roots and remind ourselves of the benefits behind the actions that will move us forward. We need to do this for those we intend to lead and inspire to positive action as well. Leaders can do more than just help team members know their why, *we can help them grow their why.*

29

Being able to help team members, coworkers, and employees - *as well as clients and prospects* – uncover and strengthen how they will be able to move forward by partnering or following us is a major key to Progress Leadership.

There is always some movement, but it is not always forward. Strengthen your commitment by continually reminding your team of the personal benefits that reaching your organization's goals will have in their lives.

Commit to Progress Leadership. *Be Progress.*

Ponder & Progress:
Internalized Reasons Create Movement

1. What are the reasons behind your team's goals?
2. How are these reasons propelling action?
3. How can you encourage all to become more motivated and bound to team goals?
4. How can you help your team discover, realize, and embrace their own reasons for action?
5. What is your WHY? What are their WHYs?
6. What are the reasons behind movement?
7. What strong reasons are needed to take strong actions?
8. How do you help all create inner drive?
9. What are you motivated to do? Why?
10. What are your team members motivated to do? Why?

"He who has a why to live for can bear almost any how."
— *Frederick Nietzsche*

30

Introducing the Six Ps of Progress

Here is something that all committed leaders must internalize. Everything we, as humans, do is done because we believe, consciously, or more often subconsciously, the projected consequences of those actions will be us feeling the right unique mixture of six core feelings, feelings I call The Six Ps of Progress.

The **Six Ps of Progress**   **Pleasure**
                                Prestige
                                Pain Avoidance
                                Power
                                Profit
                                Peace of Mind

We each project consequences based on past experiences, education, the influence of others, and our imagination. *Projected consequences* are the results we think will occur. We project consequences, we take the action, and then we perceive the actual consequences. The actual consequences may not be what we'd expected the consequences would be, but there are *always* consequences, and some blend of the *Six Ps of Progress* is experienced.

What makes this challenging is that feeling the right unique blend of the *Six Ps of Progress* is often not achieved when the feeling of them is the goal.
The right blend is more often <u>felt as a by-product</u> of working toward and attaining a goal. This is why we are each compelled to:
         — Strive for Significance
         — Pursue a Higher Purpose
         — Work to Progress.

Marketing and advertising professionals already know about the *Six Ps of Progress* (*though they don't call them that…yet).* Every good commercial comes down to showing how a particular product or service can help the buyer progress toward feeling pleasure, prestige, power, profit and peace of mind while also limiting or avoiding pain.

We choose from an endless list of possible actions in order to try and achieve our desired outcomes, thereby feeling the *Six Ps of Progress.* Some of these actions might include:
- *Dealing with an upset customer*
- *Hiring a new employee*
- *Firing an employee*
- *Writing a proposal*
- *Making sales calls*
- *Signing a contract*
- *Paying our taxes*
- *Sleeping*
- *Writing this book*
- *Learning a new skill*
- *Cleaning out the garage*
- *WHATEVER*

Each of these actions has positive meaning only when the person believes it will help them feel the right unique mixture of the Six Ps of Progress.

"For the meaning of life differs from man to man, from day to day and from hour to hour. What matters, therefore, is not the meaning of life in general but rather the specific meaning of a person's life at a given moment."
— *Dr. Viktor Frankl*

We are all motivated by self-interest. But this does not have to be selfish thinking. Even if our desired outcome is for someone else to feel pleasure or avoid pain, this too is connected to us feeling an empathetic mixture of pleasure, peace of mind, profit, prestige, power, and pain avoidance. If it weren't, we wouldn't act. **We give not so much out of the goodness of our hearts as for the goodness we feel in our hearts when we give.**

Most committed leaders know that giving adds great pleasure to life and that a life of serving others also offers great profit and even helps avoid pain. In fact, as we begin to understand this, we see how leaders that are the biggest givers end up with the most.

A major hurdle to *being progress* for ourselves and others is that nothing actually <u>causes</u> someone to feel the *Six Ps of Progress.* Products, services, ideas, and organizations can *offer* pleasure, peace of mind, profit, prestige, pain avoidance, and power. But they do not inherently *cause* it, just like nothing exterior actually *causes* stress or happiness.

What brings peace or prestige to you might not do it for me. For example: *How much money will make you feel "in the money," or feel peace of mind?* Various studies have determined that no matter what their annual income, the majority of people say they'd be significantly happier and more content if they only had *one-third more* in salary, in their nest egg, tucked under the mattress, etc.

"A human being is a deciding being."
— *Dr. Viktor Frankl*

The fact is, feeling the Six Ps is entirely *an individual choice*, and with the power of choice comes the challenge to progress. It is in the ways we go about meeting this challenge to progress that we establish an action's meaning, and even the meaning of our life.

Each of us makes decisions as to whom to connect with, whom to do business with, what to invest our time in, whom to help, and whom not to help based on whether we believe, consciously or subconsciously, that these acts will bring us the right unique mixture of these *Six Ps of Progress* – short-term or long-term.

At a mostly subconscious level, we are continuously thinking to ourselves: *Does taking this action (buying this product, switching vendors, hiring this person, calling this help line, agreeing to these terms, etc.) help me move toward pleasure, peace of mind, profit, prestige, and power, or help me to avoid pain?*

And in so doing, we are basically asking ourselves:

Will taking this action lead to Progress, or will it merely lead to more change?

> **"Everything can be taken from a man but one thing: the last of the human freedoms – to choose one's attitude in any given set of circumstances, to choose one's own way."**
> — *Dr. Viktor Frankl*

Change is inevitable, progress is a choice.
Be Progress.

Dr. Viktor Frankl: Progress Agent

I came up with the _Six Ps of Progress_ after spending years aggressively researching the works of many of the world's top minds on the subjects of positive psychology, organizational culture, motivation and leadership. In my studies I found myself leaning heavily on the work of Austrian psychiatrist and neurologist Viktor Frankl, the founder of Logotherapy.

I believe it is through our desire to feel the _Six Ps of Progress_, mixed with our belief in how to feel them, that we establish what Viktor Frankl calls our "meaning" at any given moment.

Viktor Frankl, M.D., Ph.D. (1905-1997), was an Austrian neurologist, a Holocaust survivor, and one of the greatest European psychiatrists of the twentieth century. The U.S. Library of Congress named Dr. Frankl's enlightening masterpiece, _Man's Search for Meaning,_ one of the 10 books that "made the most difference in people's lives."

Dr. Frankl is the founder of logotherapy, which he derived from the words: _logos_ – Greek for _reason_ or _meaning_, and _therapy_ – Greek, meaning _I heal._ Logotherapy therefore means _"Reasons I heal" or "Healing the Meaning"_ (trippy, profound, and enlightening both ways).

The basic philosophy of logotherapy is that people have a will to find meaning and that life can have meaning under all circumstances, even the most miserable.

Each of us has the freedom, under all circumstances, to choose to find reasons to endure and progress.

"Ever more people today have the means to live, but no meaning to live for."
— *Dr. Viktor Frankl*

We have freedom to find meaning in what we do and experience. We have freedom to take a stand when faced with an unjust and possibly unchangeable situation.

We each have the power of choice to find our unique meaning in life. Frankl believed we all have more of a desire to *feel powerful* than to *obtain power* (and there is a big difference).

Frankl first used the term logotherapy in 1926, and had developed some of its basic tenets before he was sent to a Nazi concentration camp in 1942. He even had a manuscript devoted to his views sewn into the clothes he wore when he was sent there. However, the Nazis found the manuscript, so Frankl's life's work went up in flames.

Frankl knew he had valuable ideas, but no way of actually sharing them with the world. Early on in his time in the camps he decided to recreate the manuscript, and did so on scraps of paper hidden from guards.

He also used the harsh camp environment as his field study. Frankl worked passionately to prevent inmate suicide and alleviate gloom and depression in fellow prisoners.

The Nazis did not allow anyone to actively intervene in an actual suicide attempt, so Frankl's efforts were preventative and kept secret.

He found that very few of his fellow inmates *said*, *"I want to die."* Most *said* that they wanted to live, but the ones who eventually survived the camps were those who had focused reasons attached to their survival wish – loved ones to reunite with, something to work for or to look forward to. Frankl theorized that when we have enough meaning attached to an outcome, we are able to withstand the suffering related to achieving it.

Frankl's meaning, his *strong reasons* for surviving, were connected not only to his hope of reuniting with his young wife Tilly, as well as his mother, father and brother, but also to his work. He wanted to survive, had to survive, partly because he had powerful and helpful beliefs about the human condition that he needed to recreate and share with the world.

Freed after three years at Auschwitz, Dachau, and other concentration camps, he returned to Vienna and began work on a book with the literal English translation: *From Death Camp to Existentialism: A Psychiatrist's Experiences in the Concentration Camp.* (In the U.S, we call it ***Man's Search for Meaning***.)

In the book, Frankl describes *(from the unique perspective of a psychiatrist)* the horrific life of a concentration camp inmate. With this desire to feel autonomous and powerful, Progress Agents can benefit greatly from a look into Dr. Frankl's teachings.

Three Quick Progress Leadership Action Steps
from the Work of Dr. Viktor Frankl

1. Harness the Freedom of Choice.

As markets continue to fluctuate, business challenges mount, and personal issues multiply, we each have the freedom to choose our reaction. A resourceful attitude toward a challenge is essential if the challenge is to be met. Dr. Frankl's pregnant wife, his parents and brother were all killed during their incarceration in Nazi prison camps. He'd lost everything, he said, that could be taken from a person, except one thing: *"the last of the human freedoms, to choose one's attitude in any given set of circumstances, to choose one's own way."*

We each have the power to choose, but that power is wasted if we do not exercise it. In the face of inescapable uncertainty (i.e., business challenges, a slowing economy, stiff competition), **leaders committed to progress must help their team fire up the unwavering determination that comes from possessing strong reasons to overcome daily challenges.** Frankl was a man of action. He believed we must act, must do, must persist.

2. Take Responsibility for Actions.

Frankl taught that life has an urgency to which people must respond if decisions are to be meaningful. Each of us must take responsibility for where we are in our financial situation, in our relationships, and in our career, because it is our decisions that put us there. We have the power of choice and are responsible for those choices.

We have not only a right, but a responsibility, to fulfill our individual potential, according to Frankl. **Leaders committed to progress help team members fulfill their individual potential.**

Frankl discovered that it is not what happens to us that matters. It is how we respond to what happens that is significant. Same with business. We cannot control all the elements of our personal life or business.
- Companies merge.
- Rent goes up.
- Computers crash.
- Team members retire.
- Global pandemics occur.
- Venders go out of business.
- Competitors become more competitive.
- Sales and prospecting methods evolve.
- New regulations go into effect.
- New marketing methods emerge.
- _____ *(fill in the blank)*

Leaders committed to progress help team members internalize that the only things we can control are our responses, our decisions, our actions. Our actions are our responsibility.

3. Drive Actions by Understanding Goals and Strengths.
Gaining insight into a person's reasons *(especially our own)* goes a long way in helping them progress and reach their full potential. Frankl believed in endurance, but not just for the sake of survival. He believed that all life is shot through with significance, and that this inherent meaningfulness should motivate humans to live and discover that meaning.

39

Those who have suffered loss due to injustice (racial profiling, crime), circumstance (accidents, economy, acts of nature), or the inhumanity of fellow humans know that the search for meaning is not stopped by setbacks. In many cases, as in Frankl's, challenges and adversities serve to inspire and redirect a more determined search for meaning.

> **"Life can be pulled by goals just as surely as it can be pushed by drives."**
> — *Dr. Viktor Frankl*

Leaders committed to progress understand the necessity of discovering what their followers are made of, what they're "all about." Frankl firmly believed in the great potential of his fellow humans, and stressed the ability to use one's inner resources to achieve personal goals and find personal truth.

This principle applies equally to every organization. Each member, no matter the responsibility or position, has unique strengths that can prove vital in fueling the progress of the organization.

What drives the people you hope to inspire to action? What drives you?

> **"Happiness must happen, and the same holds for success: you have to let it happen by not caring about it. I want you to listen to what your conscience commands you to do and go on to carry it out to the best of your knowledge."**
> — *Dr. Viktor Frankl*

Though much of my study of Frankl's work has been self study, I had the privilege of participating in both the Thirteenth and Seventeenth World Congresses on Viktor Frankl's Logotherapy. It was at the Thirteenth World Congress that I first met the president of the International Board of Directors of the Viktor Frankl Institute of Logotherapy, Robert Barnes, Ph.D., and his wife, Dorothy Barnes, Ed.D. (who also serves on the Institute's International Board).

I believe I was the only one at the World Congress with no letters (Ph.D., Ed.D., etc.) attached to their name. *(Well, I am a Junior, but Jr. wasn't helpful in that group.)* The Barneses quickly befriended me and even invited me to lunch with them. Over our lunch, they showed great interest in how I came to know so much about Frankl's work and why I was attending the Congress. I told them of my studies and sheepishly shared with these two revered educators The Progress Principle, my concept of the *Six Ps of Progress.*

I also explained how I believed our desire to feel these feelings helps us establish meaning, which propels us to action. Robert smiled widely, nodded, and seemed pleased. Dorothy smiled as well, but also seemed to be mulling over the Six Ps in her brain.

Our conversation went in a couple of different directions for a while – family, travel – and then Dorothy said quite confidently, *"Dean, I believe you are on to something with your Six Ps of Progress and here's why. For several years, I had wanted to lose a few pounds. However, it wasn't until Robert and I began to discuss the need to have a 30th wedding anniversary portrait taken that I actually took action.*

41

The reason I finally took action was that I knew the picture would get printed in the paper because it was our 30th, and I knew the whole community, as well as all our friends, would see it. I wanted the pleasure and prestige connected with looking good in that photo. I also wanted to avoid the pain of not looking good to myself in that photo. Good work, Dean." Dr. Robert Barnes smiled again, nodded, and seemed pleased.

I, on the other hand, was stunned. *"Wow, thank you!"* I was thrilled. It was the first time someone that I was certain KNEW what they were talking about told me they thought I was on to something. I have often thought about that lunch and conversation with great gratitude. *Thank you, Dr. and Dr. Barnes.*

A few more Frankl Facts:
During his youth, he wrote to Sigmund Freud. After Freud replied, a lively correspondence developed. Viktor traveled extensively, enjoyed a lifelong passion for mountain climbing, and even obtained his pilot's license while in his sixties.

*Dr. Frankl wrote over 30 books. However, in his autobiography, Frankl writes, **"In my view, I was never a big thinker. But one thing I may have been through my life: a thorough and persistent "thinker-through."** (A thinker-through…I like that.)*

Viktor Frankl died of cardiac arrest on the 2nd of September, 1997, in Vienna, Austria, at the age of 92. Viktor Frankl was a Progress Agent!

42

Becoming a Progress Agent

The people we desire to lead (inspire to action, serve, do business with, etc.) must believe that our leadership, our initiatives, our solutions, our organization's mission & vision, our products, and our services will help them to move forward. Solid trust must be in place before we can even hope others will choose to alter their lives to include us.

Leaders must be seen as catalysts in others' progress, agents in their progress. Leaders must be *Progress Agents.*

Progress Agents practice a **"live and lead progress"** philosophy. We thrive on being able to take a challenging situation and proactively work to create outcomes that are positive for all involved (including ourselves). We consistently say and do the things that we believe will help our organizations, as well as clients and coworkers, to grow, advance, make headway, become better, make strides, and progress in this ever-changing world.

Progress Agents understand these powerful truth… **Trust is the basis for all positive long-term relationships** *(even the one we have with ourselves).* Committed leaders know that the key to Progress Leadership is to have team members *trust* that we ARE and will continue to *Be Progress* for them.

Progress Agents know that Trust is the *Promise of Progress*, but not a guarantee of progress. Trust is fragile, but is strengthened by continually being progress for ourselves and others.

43

Progress Agents learn about employees, coworkers, customers, prospects, and even friends, uncovering their unique **_parameters for progress._** The more we can get into the shoes, hearts, and heads of the people we intend to lead and inspire to positive action, the more we can know what progress means <u>to them</u>. We are then able to relate in ways that show how our initiatives, ideas, solutions, products, and services are beneficial and valuable to them.

Ponder & Progress: Uncovering Others' Parameters for Progress

1. _What does progress mean to the people you intend to lead and inspire to action?_
2. _What are they going for in life?_
3. _What are their interests?_
4. _What are their goals?_
5. _Why do they work?_
6. _What are their internalized reasons for movement?_
7. _How are their reasons propelling them into action?_
8. _How can you share how you, your organization, your leadership, your vision, guidance, strategy, communication style, products and services are progress for the people you intend to lead and inspire to positive action?_
9. _How can you share how your ideas, recommendations, and solutions are progress?_
10. _How can you Be Progress in their minds?_

"Forces beyond your control can take away everything you possess except one thing, your freedom to choose how you will respond to the situation."
— _Dr. Viktor Frankl_

The Six Ps of Progress

"Strong reasons make strong actions."
— *William Shakespeare*

Pleasure

Leaders who truly care about the well-being of the people they lead, fair pricing, friendly polite coworkers and customer-service representatives, clean stores _(inside and out)_, humor, good hygiene and solid eye contact all act to encourage others to feel pleasure. Pleasure is a state of happiness, gratification, delight, joy, gladness, satisfaction.

> **"Pleasure in the job puts perfection in the work."**
> — _Aristotle_

Pleasure can come in mental, physical, sensual, or emotional experiences. Pleasure can come from worldly or frivolous delights, recreation, amusement, even diversions. There can be pleasure in achievement and in having done something "good."

A challenge to offering pleasure is that it is derived from _one's own_ liking, as are all the _Six Ps of Progress_. Pleasure can be promoted in countless ways, depending on how a person senses the feeling of pleasure.

Some individuals feel pleasure or happiness through personal recognition, comfort, entertainment, games, hobbies, accomplishment, and service. Music, writing, jogging, eating Twinkies®, and practically every other imaginable activity can bring about the feeling of pleasure. By getting to know those we to lead and inspire to positive action, we are able to share, in ways that are that healthy for them, how we offer them pleasure.

47

The Promise of Pleasure is why we – and especially customer-service reps – are encouraged to "smile into the phone." When we smile into the phone, there is a little lilt in our voice. The person on the other end of the call can hear that little lilt. That little lilt offers pleasure.

Offering the promise of pleasure is profitable. A dissatisfied (sometimes referred to as complaining) customer will explain their point in a more civil way if the person receiving the feedback is pleasurable to talk to. The opposite of pleasure is displeasure. Less-qualified competitors gain our customers purely because someone on our side was offering poor customer service, which caused the customer to feel displeasure.

There can and should be pleasure in service. Progress Agents savor the opportunity to help coworkers and employees, as well as customers, to progress. We can choose to feel pleasure from the work we do as well as the people we do it with. When traveling internationally on business, I am frequently asked, when getting my passport stamped, if I am traveling for *business or pleasure.* I am always tempted to say *Both.* I like the work I do. It brings me a great deal of pleasure. I hope yours does too.

Most of us participate best in a positive, upbeat working environment where we feel we are being heard and appreciated. *So why not create some hoopla, have some laughs?*

"There is little success where there is little laughter."
— *Andrew Carnegie*

48

Southwest Airlines is often cited as having an upbeat and caring culture. *Do you know who benefits the <u>most</u> from the Southwest Airlines culture?* Not us, though we get good pricing, friendly customer service, and on-time flights. The group that benefits *most* from the Southwest culture is the Southwest Airlines team members. They all *(well most, anyway)* really get a kick out of their jobs. They gain a great deal of pleasure (as well as the other *Ps of Progress*) from being a Southwest team member.

Southwest believes, *and rightfully so,* that if an organization truly takes care of its employees, the employees will take care of the customers. (By the way, this is good for stockholders, too.) Plus, the word is out on the street. When a Southwest employee shares where he or she works, people say, *"You work at Southwest? Cool. Great company. Seems like a fun place to work. You guys are well taken care of. You must dig it."* That not only delivers pleasure, but also prestige.

> **"Work is either fun or drudgery.
> It depends on your attitude. I like fun."**
> — *Colleen Barrett*

The exact opposite happens when an employee of more than a couple of other airlines shares the same info. It is usually followed by a sympathetic silence, and responses like, *"You guys got problems. Your executives are abusing you. Are you looking for a new job?"* Bummer. No fun. No pleasure, no prestige, little promise of progress. Little incentive to strive, to care, to try, to step up, to step out, to put one's self on the line. *Why bother?*

49

So, if you got game show it, share it. Spice it up.
Be thrilling. Have some gusto. Dare to care.
Truly care that the people who help you are
receiving pleasure in the relationship.

Are you fond of those around you?
Fake it and see what happens.
I bet they become people you're fond of.

Show others the zest you have for your work.
Zest offers pleasure. *No zest?* Find it, create it,
or move on. *Life is too short.*

> **"Happiness is really just about four things:**
> **perceived control, perceived progress,**
> **connectedness (number and depth of your**
> **relationships), and vision/meaning (being**
> **part of something bigger than yourself)."**
> — *Tony Hsieh*

I could go on and on about pleasure, but as Stendhal
(a complex and highly original French writer back in
the 19th century) wrote, *"Pleasure is often spoiled by
describing it."* I hope I didn't spoil anything for you.

Lead Progress by offering the Promise of Pleasure.
Commit to Progress Leadership. Be a Progress Agent.
Be Progress.

Ponder & Progress: The Pleasure 10

1. *How do you, your organization, your leadership, guidance, strategy, communication style, your organization's mission & vision, products and services offer others pleasure?*

2. *What pleasure is to be gained from working with you and for you?*

3. *How can you and your organization be better positioned as Agents of Pleasure in the minds of those you intend to lead and inspire to positive action?*

4. *What pleasure do you get from your work?*

5. *How is working toward your goals bringing you and your team pleasure?*

6. *How will accomplishing the goals you are committed to going to bring you and your team pleasure?*

7. *How can you help those you lead feel more pleasure in their work – and in their working relationship with you?*

8. *What aspects of employee engagement and morale would be improved if all felt more pleasure at work?*

9. *How is your organizational culture a catalyst for others to feel pleasure?*

10. *How do you offer the Promise of Pleasure?*

Prestige

We all want dignity, to feel we have the esteem of others, to feel that we are important and have influence. Few of us wish to live in obscurity or feel insignificant, and no one wants to feel mediocre. Prestige is the level of respect at which one is regarded by others.

Distinction can bring prestige. Awards, such as the Nobel, an Oscar, Employee of the Month, Customer of the Month, and MVP can elevate our standing in the eyes of others. Prizes also offer prestige. Sales awards offer prestige. *And what do many sales reps do after they win an annual sales award?* They win it again next year, or get darn close!

> **"Outstanding leaders go out of their way to boost the self-esteem of their personnel. If people believe in themselves, it's amazing what they can accomplish."**
> — *Sam Walton*

It is natural to want some proof of achievement, some way to look back and simply show someone what we did. Our elder daughter, Sofia, feels prestige from earning her black belt in Tang Soo Do; younger daughter, Ella, feels prestige from the kudos she gets on her art projects and deep wisdom & wit.

Heck, I still have my Little League baseball trophies *(I'm not presently displaying them but I might, and I sure did back in the day).*

For wins and grins, be ears and cheers. Sharing the credit leads to more credit to share. Give kudos. Prominence is good in the right doses. A little deserved fame can start a progress flame. We could all use a pat on the back. And it feels just as good to give someone else's back a pat. As Samuel Goldwyn, the G in MGM, said, *"When someone does something good, applaud! You will make two people happy."*

Get a boost from being the boost. Help people feel they have game, and help them celebrate that game. The recognition does not have to be complicated or even have an earth-shattering "WOW" factor.

However, I am not only talking about awards. Praise works, too. Compliments can offer prestige and a mental leg up*. Express a <u>sincere</u> compliment, even on little stuff.

"Your skills really made this project come together."
"You are such an incredible problem solver."
"You've got such amazing work ethic."
"Cool shoes!"

> **"Praise can be your most valuable asset as long as you don't aim it at yourself."**
> — *O.A. Battista*

<u>The Origin of a Leg Up:</u>
Our idiom "leg up" comes from receiving help when getting on a horse. Someone cups their hands, the rider puts his or her foot in there, and the helper lifts the rider up as the rider throws the other leg up and over the horse.

Something as simple as remembering and using people's names offers prestige. Everybody wants to feel the prestige of being thought of as unique, memorable, and important. A person's name is as important to them as yours is to you. Unfortunately, too many professionals have shared with me that they *can't remember* names.

I'll ask, *"You mean you meet someone one day and then you see them three weeks later and can't remember their name?"*

"No," they answer. *"People introduce themselves. I introduce myself, and then... poof! The name disappears."*

I do not think that in these cases we actually have trouble remembering names. I don't think we truly heard the name in the first place. To be able to offer the prestige that comes from using someone's name, make a point of catching and then tossing the name around in conversation.

Here is a four-step process for remembering names.

1. Right before you meet new people, **Focus.** Prepare to catch their name. If you do not catch it, ask them to repeat   it rather than letting it go. Do not be embarrassed to ask. *(They probably did not catch your name, either.)*
2. Casually toss their name back in your first or second response.
3. Mention their name *naturally* throughout the conversation but **DO NOT overuse it.**
4. Repeat their name when parting.

Over the centuries, there have been countless successful business leaders, but perhaps none as skilled at recognizing and rewarding team members as Mary Kay Ash, founder of Mary Kay Inc.

"Everyone has an invisible sign hanging from their neck saying, 'Make me feel important.' Never forget this message when working with people."
— *Mary Kay Ash*

Having enjoyed the privilege of working with this dazzling organization a few times over the years, I couldn't help but notice that it is an organization built on prestige. Mary Kay Ash was a strong believer in rewarding top sales professionals with what she called *"Cinderella gifts."*

These awards, or "gifts," not only included vacations and diamonds but also one of the most recognizable – and certainly most mobile – symbols of a Mary Kay sales pro's accomplishments – the pink Cadillac! Mary Kay's pink Cadillac is the sales trophy that you drive around! *It's The Prestigemobile, literally prestige on wheels!*

And the prestige just keeps on rolling. In the parking lot of Mary Kay's corporate headquarters north of Dallas, Texas, the parking spaces nearest to the front entrance to the building are not reserved for VP of Finance, VP of Marketing, or VP of Pink Dye.

They are each *Reserved for Pink Cadillac.*
If an independent Mary Kay consultant up in Oregon earns a pink Cadillac, she can *drive that sucker down and that's her spot.* Talk about prestige.

Since the Mary Kay Career Car program started in 1969, over 10,000 independent sales-force members in the United States have earned the privilege of driving a Mary Kay pink Caddy. In the company's international markets, sales professionals earn access to other model cars, including Mercedes and BMW. In all, more than 25,000 women worldwide have earned the use of a Mary Kay Career Car.

> **"No matter how busy you are, you must take time to make the other person feel important."**
> — *Mary Kay Ash*

Here is some background: In 1963, after "retiring" from a successful 25-year career in direct sales, Mary Kay Ash, a single mother of three, took her life savings of $5,000 and founded Mary Kay Cosmetics. From Day One, she passionately encouraged the independent business owners who sold her products to recognize others' accomplishments, no matter how small.

It was in this recognition-focused environment that the company went from its lean, but not mean, beginnings in a 500-square-foot Dallas storefront, to an international cosmetic dynamo.

The Mary Kay business model is simple: it is direct sales. Independent sales representatives purchase products from Mary Kay Inc. at wholesale prices and sell them directly to consumers at retail prices. Prestige-generating recognition works. Mary Kay Inc. has averaged double-digit growth each year since it was founded. *(That's sure worth a pat on the back.)*

Mary Kay products are sold in over 35 markets worldwide, including Australia *(their first international market)*, Brazil, India, Sweden, and Uruguay, with the company's top international markets being China, Russia, and Mexico. The company's global independent sales force is over 1.8 million strong.

Give prestige, get prestige. Mary Kay Ash was awarded many highly prestigious honors herself. Highlights include Baylor University hailing her as the *"Greatest Female Entrepreneur in American History,"* and being listed as one of *"America's 25 Most Influential Women"* by the *World Almanac* and *Book of Facts*. In 2004, PBS and the Wharton School of Business named Mary Kay Ash one of the *"25 Most Influential Business Leaders of the Past 25 Years."*

> **"We treat our people like royalty.**
> **If you honor and serve the people who**
> **work for you, they will honor and serve you."**
> — *Mary Kay Ash*

When I see a person driving a Mary Kay Pink Caddy, I know that person is rocking. They have game. They are leading and being *progress for* a bunch of people. The pink caddy is **proof of progress.** This is an organization based on praise and recognition, an organization, as Mary Kay Ash often said, *"with heart."* Mary Kay Ash is a stellar example of a leader committed to progress. Mary Kay Ash is a true Progress Agent.

Lead Progress by offering the Promise of Prestige. Commit to Progress Leadership. Be a Progress Agent. *Be Progress.*

Ponder and Progress: The Prestige 10

1. How do you, your organization, your leadership, guidance, strategy, communication style, your organization's mission & vision, products and services offer others prestige?

2. What prestige is to be gained from working with you and for you?

3. How can you and your organization be better positioned as Agents of Prestige in the minds of those you intend to lead and inspire to positive action?

4. How important is prestige to you? To your team members? To your prospects, clients and customers?

5. How will accomplishing the goals you are committed to going to bring you and your team prestige?

6. How is working toward your goals bringing you and your team prestige?

7. How can you help encourage and inspire coworkers and employees by offering prestige for accomplishing individual and team goals?

8. What aspects of employee engagement and morale would be improved if all felt more prestige at work?

9. How is your organizational culture a catalyst to help others to feel prestige?

10. How do you offer the Promise of Prestige?

Pain Avoidance

Wow, we have an awful lot of words for pain:
*Disappointment, Despair, Cramp, Torment, Regret,
Stress, Worry, Irritation, Shock, Woundedness,
Affliction, Bother, Agony, Suffering, Bitterness,
Distress, Headache, Heartache, Grief, Crick, Sting,
Hurt, Punishment, Misery, Aversion, Harm, Disgust,
Ache, Discomfort, Trouble, Sadness, Anxiety,
Tribulation, Woe, Distaste, Unpleasantness,
Annoyance, Boredom, Drag, Anguish, Nuisance.*

We have darting pain, sharp pain, shooting pain.
Pain can be physical (nausea, sore back, an itch) or
mental (anxiety, hatred, even boredom). We each feel
pain during our lives. The feeling of pain is one of the
main factors that organize meaning in our world and
psyche. Therefore, pain avoidance is a key pursuit.

> **"The aim of the wise is not to secure
> pleasure but to avoid pain."**
> — *Aristotle*

Social services, humanitarian aid, public-health
initiatives, community development, economic aid,
human rights programs, disaster relief, and pretty
much all forms of philanthropy are all ways to help
people avoid, prevent, or relieve pain. Scientists work
to end disease, parents pass down tools to their
children for coping with life's challenges, musicians
even write songs that help take our minds off our
daily worries and thus avoid pain. A good health-
benefits package is a pain-avoidance package.
Good fire departments, the right pair of shoes,
and toothpaste with fluoride all offer pain avoidance.

61

So do homes in safe neighborhoods, foods with low LDL cholesterol, vehicles with anti-lock brakes, vitamins, exercise equipment, and good mortgage rates. Well-trained, highly motivated, and professionally led armed forces offer pain avoidance via the same dynamics as a well-trained, highly motivated, and professionally led customer-service department. And the list goes on.

The marketing campaigns for many everyday products are built around encouraging us to view the products as solid ways to avoid pain.

Consider Calgon bath products, for example.
Their slogan is: *Take Me Away.* Their website is even TakeMeAway.com. *Away from what?*
Away from our stresses, away from our pressures, away from pain. We all have escape mechanisms or strategies for avoiding unpleasantness.

Why do people avoid an annoying or troublesome whiner or blowhard? Because they are painful to be around. (Heck, we even call them a "pain in the neck.")

"Pain leadership" and punitive pain-parenting are, unfortunately, common motivational strategies.
A dock in pay, the risk of getting fired, being grounded, no internet for a month, are all ways of communicating: *If you want to avoid pain, do what I want you to do*!

**"You don't lead by hitting people over the head –
that's assault, not leadership."**
— *Dwight D. Eisenhower*

Reminders of past pain serve as motivators as well. Coaches show players footage of a painful team defeat to inspire them to play their best so they won't feel the agony of defeat again. We all want to avoid pain, but often we don't fully consider the consequences of actions or inactions that will be painful in the long term. Consider: *What's more painful for you: Self-Discipline or Regret?*

> **"And there ain't nothing like regret to remind you you're alive."**
> — *Sheryl Crow*

If we can feel the future pain now in enough detail, then we will be compelled to do everything and anything to avoid that pain in the future – i.e., we will work toward achieving the goal. Sometimes choosing to go through pain is smart, but it still smarts. Paying our insurance premium is not painless, but most would agree that not having insurance would be more painful.

Prospecting, dealing with demanding customers, or getting up to speed on new organization products can be painful. But there is also pain in not prospecting, not dealing with demanding customers, and not getting up to speed on new organization products.

Each individual's attitude toward pain varies greatly, depending on whether the person deems the pain useless or useful, unavoidable or avoidable, unacceptable or acceptable, even undeserved or deserved. Unmet needs stay painfully in mind. Unmet potential can be painful, too. There is pain in leaving the status quo for the unknown, in risk-taking. Therefore, it can be painful to lead progress.

Some risks are worth taking, others not. Each of us gets to decide. As Progress Agents, we should be able to show those we lead as well as prospects and coworkers how there is more pain in not going through the pain of leaving the status quo, more pain in avoiding the unknown, more pain in the risk not taken.

> **"Pain in this life is not avoidable,**
> **but the pain we create**
> **avoiding pain is avoidable."**
> — *R.D. Laing*

For many years now, I have facilitated a goal-commitment program based on my book, *How to Achieve Big PHAT Goals.* PHAT is a slang acronym that stands for Pretty, Hot, And Tempting. Basically, PHAT means attractive.

Our personal and professional goals have to be attractive to us if we are going to be committed to them. Our products and services have to be attractive to clients and prospects if they are going to commit their money and time. Likewise, our ideas and initiatives have to be attractive to those we'd like to see involved in their implementation.

Once early in my career, after presenting a speech on goal commitment to a group of area business owners, I caught the eye of an extremely fit man standing ramrod straight and tall. Sporting a crew cut, polished army boots, camouflage pants, and a dark green monogrammed T-shirt, he really stood out *(not your normal attire for this type of function).*

64

We nodded to each other and I could tell by his body language that he was waiting for the right moment to come speak with me. After several other participants and I had discussed my speech and some opportunities, the gentleman walked up to me, coming to a stop just a little closer to me than was normal.
In a commanding but not loud voice he said, *"Dean?"*
I responded, almost instinctively, *"Yes, sir!"*

He said, *"I've got a military background."*
I said, *"Yes, sir. I could tell, sir."*

He said, *"Drill sergeant, eight years. I now run a fitness boot camp. Good speech. I'd like to have you present your Big PHAT program to my cadets next Saturday."*
At this point in my business career I did not need to check my calendar. *"Yes, sir."*

He continued, *"Why don't you come by next Tuesday evening? We can discuss the program and I'll give you a tour of the campus. You'll get a chance to meet some of the cadets and we can get them worked up about the workshop."*

"Yes, sir," I said. Again, no calendar required.
He told me he had rented some warehouse space on the outskirts of town for his campus, and that his cadets arrived at 5:40 p.m. and drills started at 6:00 p.m. sharp. I arrived at his place that next Tuesday at 5:15 p.m.

I walked into what seemed like a normal office.
He greeted me and spent several minutes discussing why he was interested in the workshop.

65

The drill sergeant shared his desire to help his cadets reach their fitness goals, and that he believed the Big PHAT Goals program could help. He understood that each of us commits to a goal with strong reasons and the best of intentions. But without constant reinforcement, our strong reasons can weaken over time to the point where some other action becomes more attractive.

We discussed how each of us is continuously motivated to do one thing or another (get up, sleep in. Eat the cheesecake, not eat the cheesecake). Consciously or subconsciously, we are constantly deciding that some outcomes are more attractive or more tempting than others, and we act accordingly. I could relate. For decades, I had the habit of setting a New Year's resolution to lose weight.

Each year I would get myself a fitness membership and work out a few times, only to stumble back into my "normal" routine. I never forgot that I wanted to be skinny, but I did lose sight of why I wanted to be skinny. There were so many other things that I could choose to do with that time.

As we talked, I quickly realized the drill sergeant caught the concept of using the Six Ps of Progress to propel action. He understood that we needed to help his cadets truly internalize the reasons behind their movements and offer them tools to help them stay committed to their goals.

"Dean, let me show you the campus," he said.
"Yes, Sir!!" I had been wondering about this campus.

He opened up the back door to the office, revealing a long thin room with a concrete floor and a metal roof. Calling the sarge's campus "old school" would be a stretch. I doubt he had invested more than seventy-five dollars outfitting the whole place. He had drilled holes in the concrete walls and stuck in metal poles for pull-ups.

Concrete blocks with twine handles served for curls, and sheets of cardboard in one corner marked the spot where cadets did their sit-ups and their push-ups. He'd even mowed a half-mile running track though the fields and woods behind the warehouse (I mean, *campus)*. This was definitely not Life Time Fitness.

I was really curious about what type of people were enrolled in the drill sergeant's boot camp. Then they started to arrive. They were regular people! Good, solid, hardworking folks (like us); a few still had their badges on from the places where they worked.

And he treated them like normal people, until the first one came out of the changing room wearing bright orange shorts and a gray shirt. (Turns out everyone had matching bright orange shorts and gray shirts. Pause a second to get the visual.)

When the last cadet came out in her attire, the drill sergeant reached into the bottom drawer of his desk and pulled out his drill sergeant hat, one of those *Smokey the Bear Meets Full Metal Jacket* hats with the hard brim that goes all the way around.

As soon as the hat hit his head, his intensity went to 11. He barked, *"All right. Let's go, grunts!"*

In a flash, they all ran out the back door to the track. About ten minutes later, the drill sergeant marched his cadets back in. Each was breaking a pretty decent sweat. Meanwhile, the sergeant was still barking orders, now mixed with song lyrics: *"Pick up that concrete, put it down. Go over there and give me fifteen. Gotta get up to get down, my little grunts. Gotta get up to get down. Chin up!"*

This guy was a trip. He got right up in their faces, then suddenly yelled, *"Grunts to the mat and sit!"*

They knew exactly what that meant. The cadets all scrambled over to the cardboard and sat down, Indian style. They were panting and wiping sweat from their eyes. After pacing in front of them for about a minute, he waved me over. *"C'mon over here, big PHAT guy."*

I know what you're thinking: "Big PHAT Guy" – not a great moniker. But hey, it's branding, and at that point in my career I was glad to be known as anything. So I was the Big PHAT guy. *"Come over here, Big PHAT guy. Tell us about your awesome program to help my cadets stick to their guns."*

As I walked over to them, I could have sworn I saw a couple of them mouth, *"Thank you"* to me for getting them a break. I did not aspire to match the drill sergeant's presentation style, so I asked plainly, with little emotion, *"How many of you are here to avoid pain?"*

The cadets looked confused by the question and no one raised their hand. They were in pain. Couldn't I see that?

68

How could they be going through this boot camp to avoid pain? I asked again, *"How many are here to avoid pain?"*

The drill sergeant raised his hand. I said, *"Yes, sir?"* He said, *"My cadets are here to avoid pain – let there be no doubt. My cadets feel pain in not being able to fit into anything in their closet, not being able to walk up a flight and a half of stairs without huffing and puffing. "* He continued, *"Some even worry about dying from a heart pain before their kids graduate from high school. My painful boot camp helps them avoid that pain."*

The cadets stared at the drill sergeant for a few seconds and then, one by one, each started nodding in agreement. I could see a sense of purpose build in their eyes. They were there to avoid pain.

The Big PHAT Goals program the following Saturday was well attended, and every one of the drill sergeant's "grunts" participated (maybe they were scared not to).

The cadets made lists of the pain they were working to avoid by being in the boot camp. Items included diabetes, joint and back pain, personal disappointment, and loneliness.

Though the program was many years ago, one of the drill sergeant's grunts recently contacted me to share that she still reads over her list to keep herself attracted to her fitness goals.

Lead Progress by offering the Promise of Pain Avoidance. Commit to Progress Leadership. Be a Progress Agent. *Be Progress.*

Ponder & Progress:
The Pain Avoidance 10

1. How do you, your organization, your leadership, guidance, strategy, communication style, your organization's mission & vision, products and services offer others pain avoidance?

2. What pain is to be avoided by working with you and for you?

3. How can you and your organization be better positioned as Agents of Pain Avoidance in the minds of those you intend to lead and inspire to positive action?

4. What is more painful to you – <u>self-discipline</u> or <u>regret</u>?

5. How is working toward your goals helping you and your team avoid pain?

6. How will accomplishing the goals you are committed to going to help you and your team avoid pain?

7. How can you better share how you offer pain avoidance to prospects, clients, and customers?

8. What aspects of employee engagement and morale would be improved if all felt more pain avoidance at work?

9. How is your organizational culture a catalyst to help others to avoid pain?

10. How do you offer the Promise of Pain Avoidance?

Power

When considering the meaning of power, many words come to mind: *clout, brawn, capacity, ability, might, influence, muscle, steam, horsepower, leadership.* But the word that sums up the true feeling of power is the word **Choice**, the power to determine our own thoughts and actions.

"Between stimulus and response there is a space. In that space is our power to choose our response. In our response lies our growth and our freedom."
— *Dr. Viktor Frankl*

Who has power? Everyone. Each of us has the power of choice. We each hold the power of decision making. Even self-discipline is flexing our power of choice *(mind over ice cream)*.

Power is not just enforcement. In the form of influence and persuasion, power is used in countless ways to encourage people to choose to act, feel, and behave in ways other than how they may have initially planned, or would habitually react.

Each of us would make different choices if we were influenced differently. In essence, all human interaction involves power, because ideas hold power, and ideas underlie all language and action.

There is power in branding. There is power in marketing, in PR, in advertising. There is power in "word of mouth" and in social influence. There is power in shared beliefs. Expertise offers power. Training leads to power. Degrees can translate as power.

Positions can hold power. Power is exercised when 'we are able to reward and promote. Wealth can bring power. Some feel power from being accepted. Education offers the promise of power because it 'builds the mental qualities and knowledge to make choices that get things done.

But it is not only knowledge that offers power; being able to communicate knowledge is also power. It is not just what we know or whom we know; it is mainly what we decide to DO with what we know that is paramount.

Power is the ability (present or anticipated) to make choices that bring about significant *change*, usually in people's lives, through one's own actions or those of others. *Nengli*, the Mandarin word for power, literally means "can-strength," or "being capable."

To lead others, one must have some understanding and mastery of the situations or things the other person desires or needs. A boss, manager, or employer wields power over employees because he or she commonly controls projects, working conditions, wages, hiring and firing, etc.

However, employees hold power, too. They can quit, slack off, form a union, steal pens and toilet paper, undermine coworkers' morale, provide lousy service, and be all-out liabilities.

Employees can also arrive on time, be supportive team players, think outside of the box, and provide world-class service. It all comes down to the power of choice.

All parties in all relationships have some power. Customers have power to choose to spend their money wherever they please. Companies have the power to alter policies or refuse service. Power can be delegated, but only to those who choose to accept the power.

One primitive but common way of obtaining the feeling of power is by threatening someone with pain *(firing, a bonk on the head, no dessert)*. There is power in threatening pain. But this kind of thought and behavior is a misuse of power and is often counterproductive.

As any student of world history or "office politics" will tell you, such "power" inevitably builds resentment and resistance. And, there is power in resistance. *"Fight the Power"* is itself a statement of power.

Someone's awareness of us and our abilities can have powerful results. People carry archives of knowledge and impressions within their gray matter, and it behooves us to have ourselves archived as a source of power. Powerful people are those with easy access to resources, those who can reliably exercise their will, their ideas, and their way.

Progress Agents are able to show how the choices we want others to make will bring them more choices, more power, more progress. But it is still each individual's choice as to what to think and believe, and how to act.

Lead Progress by offering the Promise of Power. Commit to Progress Leadership. Be a Progress Agent. *Be Progress.*

73

Ponder & Progress: The Power 10

1. How do you, your organization, your leadership, guidance, strategy, communication style, your organization's mission & vision, products and services offer others power?

2. What power is to be gained from working with you and for you?

3. How can you and your organization be better positioned as Agents of Power in the minds of those you intend to lead and inspire to positive action?

4. How will you remind yourself that you always have the power of choice even in uncomfortable or negative situations?

5. How is working toward your goals bringing you and your team power?

6. How will accomplishing the goals you are committed to going to bring you and your team power?

7. What in particular does your product or service enable people to do that they could not otherwise do?

8. What aspects of employee engagement and morale would be improved if all felt more power at work?

9. How is your organizational culture a catalyst for others to feel powerful?

10. How do you offer the Promise of Power?

Profit

Most of us think "revenue" when we think profit.
Therefore, it is helpful to include the terms *money*
and *sales* when discussing the concept of feeling profit.
"Nothing happens until someone sells something" is
a dead-on classic business truism. On some level,
all leaders are in sales. We all *sell* something –
our leadership, our organizations, our vision, our ideas,
our products, our services, our old refrigerator,
our version of progress. A job interview is a sales call;
so is a date. Sales is NOT a dirty word. Sales is
the art of influence.

Sure, profit means *dinero* (Spanish for money), *geld*
(German for money), and *pengar* (Swedish for money).
But profit can also mean to prosper, to gain an
advantage, or to improve. **I even learned while doing
research for this book that the word *profit* comes
from a Latin word meaning "to make progress."
*Cool, huh?***

So much of life is perception: perceived benefits,
perceived value, and perceived profit. Coworkers and
employees need to perceive that the organization they
work for (partner with) is heading in a direction that will
be profitable for them. Likewise, prospects and
customers need to perceive through our guidance and
education that our product or service will fill their
needs, meet their requirements, help them profit.

The promise of profit helps form expectations.
To encourage productivity and employee retention,
and even customer loyalty and quality referrals we
must exceed expectations or at least match them.

75

So, what do team members and customers expect?
Everyone is different, but we can assume we all want caring competent leaders, a positive work environment, a respectable wage, quality products and solid customer service. As customers, we also want the products and services a Progress Agent in Sales (Read: Sales Professionals) recommends to actually be in our best interests and not just what the organization is pushing this week, or those with the best profit margin.

> **"Profit is the celebration of service."**
> — *Denis Waitley*

Employees, coworkers as well as prospects and customers, must believe they gain an upper hand* in some way from their relationship with us, our solutions and our companies. They must believe they profit from us, just as we are profiting from them.

Leaders committed being progress in an ever-changing world are in the business of sales. The business of sales is the business of attraction. We are attracted to products, services, ideas, and people that we trust can help us progress.

*The Origin of Upper Hand:
The expression "upper hand" comes from America's once-favorite pastime, baseball. To decide which team would bat first in a sandlot baseball game, one player would grab a baseball bat at its base. A player from the other team would then place his hand above the first player's hand. Up the bat they would go, each gripping the bat until they reached the top. The player with the topmost hand would then have the "upper hand," with the choice of batting first.

The days of the "Surefire Closing Statement" and the "Glad-handing Slick Salesman" are long gone. *Are we even shaking hands now?* Today it is imperative for Progress Agents in sales to truly get to know their prospects and help prospects get to know them.

The great Dottie Walters, one of the founders of the National Speakers Association, shared with me many years ago that the word <u>sales</u> comes from the Scandinavian root word meaning to serve.

Soak that in…**to serve**. If leaders could help their sales professionals make that little shift in thinking about that word *sales*, think of how many more people we could serve with solutions, products, services, ideas, and contacts. To sell is to serve, to serve is to *Be Progress.*

Selling is therefore a state of mind more than a series of steps. It is a dance, a buzz, a willingness to be involved, to connect, to attract. Those of us who make our careers selling are, by and large, outgoing, caring, and driven.

In leadership and in sales, if we want to arrive at a true WIN/WIN, first we must believe we have a WIN to offer. We must believe we can make a positive difference, that we can help. Leadership, relationship building and sales are all about trust. **Trust is the Promise of Progress.** Here are seven profitable habits for leaders in sales *(hint: all leaders are in sales).*

> **"Leadership is a series of behaviors**
> **rather than a role for heroes."**
> — *Margaret Wheatley*

1. Become Buzz-worthy.

Leaders in sales should provide so much value, so much heat, and so much enthusiasm that customers are inspired to talk about us. Be a sales leader that is worthy of attention, worthy of the spotlight, worthy of wattage, and worthy of referrals. ALL leaders, must not only show enthusiasm for our work – we must HAVE enthusiasm for our work. If we want others to get excited about our recommendations and solutions, we need to have that excitement first. Likewise, if we want others to believe in our products and services, we must believe in our products and services first.

To win the prize, we must *be* the prize. Enthusiasm shows in the way we hold ourselves and in the passion we have for our jobs and our lives. If we want loyal customers and referrals *(and we do),* then we need to feel worthy of loyal customers and referrals. I am sure you have sensed by now that, whenever possible, people do business with people they like.

Passion for our lives and belief in our work make us attractive and likable. They draw people to us.
In sales, we have got to be *on*. Have game.
Bring heat. Same is true for customer-service professionals and those in leadership. Buzz. Buzz.

2. Ask Progress-Based, Open-Ended Questions.

In the medical profession, it is known that prescription without diagnosis is malpractice. The same is true for leaders. We must ask a variety of open-ended questions to diagnose the situation, so our recommendation *(prescription)* will meet the need.

> **"The art and science of asking questions
> is the source of all knowledge."**
> — *Thomas Berger*

There is a classic story, told in sales circles, of the inept salesman trying to explain to his boss why he closed only one sale per month. *"You know, you can lead a horse to water, but you can't make him drink,"* the salesman says, shrugging his shoulders.
"Make him drink?" the manager replies.
"Your job is to make him thirsty."

That sounds good enough, but there's a fundamental oversight here: Clients and prospects are **already "thirsty."** They are thirsty for pleasure, prestige, pain avoidance, power, profit and peace of mind. They are thirsty for progress. We must uncover others' particular parameters for progress if we hope to make them thirsty for the progress we offer.

The most powerful way for a leader to uncover the team member's or prospect's parameters for progress is to ask open-ended questions. These questions commonly include the basics of: Who, What, Where, Why, When and How.

> **"The best scientists and explorers have the attributes of kids! They ask questions and have a sense of wonder. They have curiosity. 'Who, what, where, why, when and how!' They never stop asking questions, and I never stop asking questions, just like a five year old."**
> — *Sylvia Earle*

A Dozen Solid Open-Ended
Questions for Leaders in Sales

Please find your own voice when asking these questions.
We must be truly interested in finding a way to help.

1. *How* did you get interested in your line of work?
2. If a journalist were to write about what's been happening in your industry over the past six months, *what* might they write?
3. I connect with new people all the time; *how* would I know if someone qualified as a solid contact for you?
4. *How* would you define progress for you/your business?
5. *What* major shifts do you foresee in your industry?
6. *Where* do you see your greatest challenges?
7. *Why* do these challenges persist?
8. *What* difficulties will you face if you don't meet these challenges?
9. *What* actions are you taking to overcome these challenges?
10. *What* results are you expecting?
11. *Who* is involved in the decision-making process?
12. If you could solve these challenges, *what* kind of progress would you make?

Also, encourage prospects and clients to expand on their answers by asking:

> *Would you tell me more about that?*
> *Could you please elaborate?*
> *Could you clarify...?   How so?*
> *What did you mean when you said...?*

Do not ask too many questions or ask them at a rocket-fire clip. People should not feel they are being interrogated. Being interrogated is neither attractive nor enjoyable.

3. Listen as if your lifestyle depended on it…

It Does! Solid listening goes hand in hand with
asking powerful questions. I don't mean "listen"
as in taking in sounds and passively processing them.
As leaders, we must LISTEN with all we've got.
This is a basic but sometimes challenging principle
to consistently put into practice. It means that, for the
duration of our contact, we step outside of ourselves –
our own needs, our every preconception - and attend
entirely to someone else.

Everyone has a need to talk and be heard.
Listening helps us treat others as if they were the
most important people on the planet because –
in their minds – they *are*. Many professionals forget
to involve others and drone on about how great their
ideas or their organization is, forgetting to ask probing
questions and listening for ways to show how they
can be progress for the other person.

Sometimes our motivation to actively listen is not
all that high. We think we can get by without really
focusing. This is a huge mistake. The ability to
understand and value what others say is critical to
being a leader committed to being progress in an
ever-changing world. So be determined to focus
on and understand completely what others are
trying to communicate.

It is close to impossible to uncover someone's
parameters of progress when you're preoccupied
with previous conversations, unfinished tasks, or
the impression you're making. Good listeners
absorb and reflect on what they hear. They are
active in the listening process.

This requires energy and motivation, because listening is more than just hearing. We must become active listeners rather than passive hearers. Repeating back (as questions or tentative statements) what you think you've heard the other person say helps avoid mind-misreading errors. Good clarifying questions offer the person a chance to rephrase their thoughts and say precisely what they mean.

4. Respect Time and Structure. Structure is mission critical. Solid self-management leads to higher productivity and reduced stress. Our desks need to be workstations, not storage space. We must be able to quickly locate important information. Being well organized shows a respect for time (ours, our team members' and our customers').

Looking sharp is also part of solid organization. If we can't get ourselves together well enough to look presentable, *how are we going to be able to help someone else see us as together enough to handle their challenges?* Plus, how we present ourselves shouts volumes about how we feel about ourselves and our work. Becoming a leader in sales takes preparation. Unfortunately, far too many of us invest more energy in planning our weekends, or even what we'll have for dinner, than we do our opportunities to be progress for prospects and customers.

Don't believe anyone who says sales is *"just a numbers game."* Sales is a Progress-based Impressions Game – a Proof-of-Progress Game – The Ultimate Game of Trust.

Sure, the more contacts you make the better your odds – but you may also be blowing your chances for many potential relationships, not to mention time (yours and the prospect's), by rushing through the process half-cocked with an indifferent attitude. The worst time to think of what you're going to say is as it's coming out of your mouth.

Ponder & Progress: Sales & Organization
Consider your three most recent sales presentations or sales phone calls:

1. *Did you check your attitude before making contact?*
2. *Did you have a specific objective for the contact?*
3. *Did you have some ideas to offer on how you could Be Progress?*
4. *What was your plan?*
5. *Did you know what you were going to say?*
6. *Did you do enough research?*
7. *Did you set an appointment?*
8. *Were your materials in order?*
9. *Were your questions relevant and helpful?*
10. *Was the person inspired to positive action?*

Bonus Question:
Did you make a sale or start a progress-based relationship?

Prepare, keep your enthusiasm, and be persistent. Eighty percent of new sales are made on the fifth contact, yet the majority of salespeople give up after the second contact. Give full attention to every relationship opportunity.   Being well organized makes it easier to build trust and offer progress.

5. Build Priceless Business Relationships

Building priceless business relationships does NOT hinge on who we know, or even who knows us.
The key to building priceless business relationships is to proactively use what we know about who we know so that we can position ourselves as progress in the minds of those we intend to build priceless business relationships with. Follow this networking CODE.

The Progress Agents' Networking CODE:
4 Steps to Priceless Business Relationships

Create Strong Belief in Self and Services
Open Face-to-Face Relationships
Deliver Strong First Impressions
Earn Trust

"Sometimes, idealistic people are put off the whole business of networking as something tainted by flattery and the pursuit of selfish advantage. But virtue in obscurity is rewarded only in Heaven. To succeed in this world you have to be known to people."
— *Sonia Sotomayor*

6. Practice Empathy.

Empathy is knowing and feeling where the other person is coming from, walking a mile in their shoes, seeing things from their point of view. Empathy involves understanding that people make decisions for their own reasons, not ours. There are always reasons. Customers have reasons, prospects have reasons, employees have reasons, coworkers have reasons. They might not be our reasons. To enhance our level of empathy, it is paramount to focus on understanding others' parameters for progress.

84

We may never fully uncover where another person's motivation, their *"motives for actions,"* are coming from, but those motives, along with their parameters for progress, are uniquely theirs.

> **"I know it might sound weird, but empathy**
> **is one of the greatest creators of energy.**
> **It's counterintuitive because it's selfless."**
> — *Angela Ahrendts*

To be a Progress Agent, always think, and say: *"What that means to you, Mrs./Mr. Prospect, is…"* Commit to doing what is best for the customer, ever striving to help provide the right product or service to meet their needs. Sure, we want to profit, but the customer's profit is key to ours. Practicing empathy includes understanding that customers do not want our products and services – they want what they think our products and services can do for them.

One of my client companies is among the largest trade show booth manufacturers in the USA. They design, build, and transport the huge trade show booths you see at the big conferences around the country and world. At the very beginning of a program I was conducting for their sales teams, I stated bluntly, *"No one wants a trade booth."*

The room went silent. The reps looked at the Vice President of Sales and each other as if to say, *"What?"*

Finally, one of the sales managers in the back raised his hand and said, *"No, Dean. They actually call us up and order trade show booths."*

I said, *"You bet. They order trade show booths, but a trade show booth is not really what they want."* Again, more silence.

Then the Vice President of Sales spoke. *"You're right, Dean. Our customers don't want trade show booths – they want profit. We must be able to show them how investing in our trade show booths will help them to profit."*

Leaders in sales know it is not the goal of having the product or service itself that creates the momentum. It is the perceived benefits (feelings realized) behind having or utilizing the product or service that creates the momentum.

7. Focus on Value and Cost, Not Price.
Sure, it is easy for prospects, as well as sales professionals, to focus on price because it's right there in black and white. And true, our products and services do come with a price.

Remember, the *price* of a product or service isn't what the product or service actually *costs*.

We must show that every penny of the price is necessary, because it offers the best **VALUE** and avoids the cost of alternative purchases and unwanted situations & setbacks.

> **"Too many people today know the price of everything and the value of nothing."**
> — *Ann Landers*

86

Cost and value are hard to nail down but are far more important figures to relate – because they include not only the price, but also the value-added service, technical support, our expertise, and all the other progress-based aspects that go along with a relationship with us and our organization.

There are often ramifications from purchasing-decisions that are eventually felt within other departments. True value shows itself over time. The challenge and responsibility of a sales professional is to relay the true costs of other choices upfront. Buyers must see that they profit by investing their time and money with us.

"Our prices are too high" is often the excuse heard from sales professionals as they explain their less-than-stellar sales performance. Sometimes it's true. Most of the time, however, the issue is not our price; it's articulating the true cost, and how working with us and agreeing to our price is the best value option and therefore means progress. If prospects have a strong enough why, they will figure out the how.

If employees have a strong enough why, they too will figure out the how. When things get tough, reminding coworkers, employees, and ourselves of the progress behind the desired actions is paramount.

Lead Progress by offering the Promise of Profit. Commit to Progress Leadership. Be a Progress Agent. *Be Progress.*

Ponder and Progress: The Profit 10

1 How do you, your organization, your leadership, guidance, strategy, communication style, your organization's mission & vision, products and services offer others profit?

2. What profit is to be gained from working with you and for you?

3. How can you and your organization be better positioned as Agents of Profit in the minds of those you intend to lead and inspire to positive action?

4. How can you help all involved focus on <u>cost</u>, not price?

5. How is working toward your goals bringing you and your team profit?

6. How will accomplishing the goals you are committed to going to bring you and your team profit?

7. How do you profit from better teamwork and by helping your organization *profit and become more productive?*

8. What aspects of employee engagement and morale would be improved if all felt more profit at work?

9. How is your organizational culture a catalyst for others to feel they are profiting?

10. How do you offer the Promise of Profit?

Peace of Mind

If I had to choose one of the *Six Ps of Progress* that was the most often strived for, it would be Peace of Mind. In simple terms, *peace of mind* is acceptance and contentment. Peace of mind means inner calmness, quiet mind, serenity, a clear conscience, safety, composure, contentment. It also means an absence of mental stress or anxiety, a lack of agitation. (Sounds nice, huh?)

Peace of mind is the state of tranquility and harmony, sleeping easy at night, living easy during the day. When I think of an example of someone who seems to enjoy peace of mind, I think of Jimmy Buffett. I am sure Jimmy has had a bad day here and there, even in Margaritaville, but I have a hard time imagining him not eventually finding that lost shaker of salt – or at least taking its loss with a grain of salt.

"Every goal, every action, every thought, every feeling one experiences, whether it be consciously or unconsciously known, is an attempt to increase one's level of peace of mind."
— *Sidney Madwed*

Solid caring leadership offers peace of mind. Strong business relationships offer peace of mind. Insurance offers peace of mind. Good benefit packages offer peace of mind. Money in the bank offers peace of mind. Good buzz in our industries offers peace of mind. Meaningful work offers peace of mind. Seatbelts offer peace of mind. Receiving solid customer service offers peace of mind.

In equal measure, I strongly believe that *delivering* solid customer service offers peace of mind. Most would agree that having peace of mind is healthy and the opposite of being anxious or burdened with regret and worry. Understanding that unexpected things will happen, markets shift, wells dry up – and that all we truly control is our actions and reactions – offers peace of mind. We have the best shot at feeling peace of mind when we start viewing the world and its opportunities from a healthy and useful perspective.

Peace of mind may also relate to a state of being spiritual, or having a sense of possessing enough knowledge and understanding to keep oneself positive and centered in the face of stressful stimuli and discord. It is tough to feel peace when we are angry or upset. Forgiving both ourselves and others, as well as letting go of grudges, are prerequisites to peace of mind.

Peace of mind does not suggest lack of awareness, Pollyannaism, or loss of touch with reality. Someone with peace of mind can be extremely aware and closely connected to the reality of the times. Belief in ourselves and our abilities to make good choices despite any downturn or misstep offers peace of mind. Knowing we are doing our best at becoming our best selves is, in itself, peace of mind. Believing we can lead progress in an ever-changing world sustains our peace with courage and conviction.

"With the power of conviction there is no sacrifice."
— *Pat Benatar*

90

Peace of mind is as oxygen in the challenging world of business, especially in the area of customer service. Sure, pleasure, prestige, pain avoidance, power and profit are desired too, but first and foremost, customers need the peace and confidence that only our caring can provide. Continually showing customers that we care, are knowledgeable, and are committed to their progress is the vital force that keeps our relationships and businesses alive.

And I know what I'm talking about.
I do not wish to brag, but I am a customer.
I have been since I got my first allowance.
Heck, a couple of you may be customers too.

As customers, we want the peace of mind that comes from a customer-service representative listening to our issues and championing our cause. We want the peace of mind that comes from believing that a sales representative is acting in our best interest. We want the peace of mind that comes from employees looking and acting like they want to be there, and who are passionate about their work.

But let's not think for a minute that providing solid customer service is something done *only* for the customer. We shouldn't kid ourselves. Providing solid customer care adds to our peace of mind, too. Many of our goals are achieved by serving customers.

One of the major reasons we even wear the *"Serve others"* hat is so we can wear the *"Serve me"* hat later in the day. Our service to others, serves us. It helps to keep the personal benefits of providing unparalleled service front and center in our minds.

There are times we do not feel like serving customers, but we always want to serve ourselves. There are even times when the customer (who may be surly, rude, drunk) does not deserve our best. But we always desire the best for ourselves. Therefore, it can be helpful to remind ourselves - and our team members - of the role that earning and maintaining customer loyalty plays in our personal peace of mind and progress.

Want to get closer to job security? Serve customers.
Want less stress? Provide commendable service.
Want your 401(K) to grow? Earn customer loyalty.
Worried about downsizing? Serve customers.
Want your organization *to be more profitable?* Ditto.
Want to have more fun at work? Serve those bosses, I mean customers, patrons, guests, I mean bosses!
Want team members to be more focused on your organization's mission and vision? Focus on providing outstanding <u>internal</u> customer service.
Want job satisfaction? Serve.
Want your customers to feel peace of mind? Serve.
Do you want the peace of mind that comes with customer loyalty? You guessed it...**Serve Those Customers!**

Progress Agents help all team members internalize the fact and consistently act with the understanding that customers are: **Revenue, Referrals & Reality.**

> **"If you're not serving the customer, your job is to be serving someone who is."**
> — *Jan Carlzon*

Offering team members, prospects and customers the promise of peace of mind, offers us peace of mind. That is why we strive for employee and customer loyalty, so that we KNOW we have a team - and a customer base - that is solid, jazzed, and growing. That knowledge sure helps me sleep well at night. *How about you?*

Service pays off – and not only in spades. In the hand that we deal are the "hearts" of much happier customers and a more satisfying workday; the "diamonds" of higher pay and lower turnover; and the "lucky" clover (club) of more sales and organizational growth. *(That was forced, but fun.)*

When we lose sight of the personal motivation involved in this game *(ok, I'll stop)* of quality service, we begin to disregard the concerns of our customers. Unfortunately for everyone, this makes them unhappy, leads to legitimate complaints, and could easily end in our looking for some other line of work. We reach our full potential when service becomes habitual.

Know let us talk specifically about customer service. Customer service is far too often a sticky slow web of surly, under-informed customer-service reps, reading in a monotone from a script. Add to that the annoying on-hold music, outdated computer programs, and hard-to-navigate Web sites (none of which offer customers peace of mind or any of the other Six Ps), and you have the perfect Rx for customer *disservice,* also known as failure. Customers with concerns are left feeling stressed and helpless, and with the belief that companies truly don't give a hoot about their well-being. No progress only change.

If we treated all our customers as if they were our best customers, we would have a lot more "best customers". Just saying we provide "great customer service" doesn't cut it anymore. Every organization says they provide *great* customer service, or *super* customer service or *stellar* customer service.

You never hear of an organization touting their lame service. *"Our customer service generally sucks. But we do have our good days, so how's about buying something?"*

Many adjectives have been plopped in front of the words "customer service" to help rally some form of interest in providing positive service to customers. They include: *Astonishing, Superior, Exceptional, Positively Outrageous, Super, Multicultural, World-Class, Magnetic, Effective, Branded, Practical, Nonpareil, Breakthrough, Remarkable, Magical, Quality, Effective, Five-Star, and So-So Service.*

(OK. I was kidding about that last one, but it does have the makings of an interesting talk: *Just Say NO to So-So Service: Breaking the 7 Habits of Barely Tolerable Service Professionals*.)

A thorough definition of *customer service* is full of intangibles, and it is those intangibles that make or break a business. In today's competitive marketplace, *service* is the most important thing an organization has to *offer*.

Progress Agents know the best marketing is a rocking customer experience!! Progress in service leads to progress in sales.

Many companies win customers with special offers, only to lose that new business to their competitor by providing lousy service. Quality customer service makes the all-important difference when two, ten, or twenty businesses seem to offer the same product or professional service. If we want our exterior customer service to be first rate, our internal customer service must be first rate first.

The need is undeniable, the concepts are easy to understand, and the training sound, but still, proactive customer service is just not happening. All expect good service but few are willing to give it. It helps to widen our perspective as to what a customer is.

Anyone affected, positively or negatively, by the work we do (including our families and ourselves) can be thought of as our "customer." Within this wider perspective, we see that real service is based on integrity, care, and sincerity, none of which can be measured with money. Nor can it be automated, no matter how soft-spoken and attractive the audio-animatronic voice may be.

Unfortunately, it seems that when an organization labels some of its professionals as *customer-service reps* or *customer advocates,* the rest of the organization assumes they are let off of the "customer care" hook. Not true. **We are ALL in the customer-service business.** There is no other business. In fact, there is NO business without the customer.

> **"The customers are the most important part of the production line."**
> — *W. Edwards Deming*

95

Every member of our organization is a "customer-service representative," no matter what their title or job description may be. We are all working for the customer *(or client, or guest, or partner, or stockholder, or employee, or team member)*. Customers are not dependent on us; we are dependent on them.
But don't get me wrong... An attitude of service is not one of servitude. It is an attitude of goodwill and good-willingness, a willingness to help others progress.

Lead Progress by offering the Promise of Peace of Mind. Commit to Progress Leadership. Be a Progress Agent. *Be Progress.*

Ponder & Progress:
Defining Your Way of Customer Care

1. *Why do you serve?*
2. *Whom do you serve?*
3. *Who are your customers? Who are not your customers?*
4. *Who should provide customer service?*
5. *How would you define customer service as a customer?*
6. *How would you define service as a business owner, customer-service representative or sales professional?*
7. *Who at your organization does not need to be focused on customer service?*
8. *What are the personal and/or shared rewards of serving customers successfully?*
9. *What are the consequences of failing to provide what the customer views as "good service?"*
10. *How is providing solid customer service progress for YOU?*

Just Say NO to So-So Service:
Breaking the 7 Habits of Barely Tolerable Service Professionals:

Here is an outline of the 7 Habits.

Habit 1:
Be Slow to React to Others' Concerns

Habit 2:
Begin with the End of the Business Day in Mind

Habit 3:
Put First Things Last and Don't Get Around to Them

Habit 4:
Think Lose/Win or Win/Lose – Somebody Has Got to Lose

Habit 5:
Seek First to Tell. Then Hang Up

Habit 6:
Scrutinize Others' Needs to See If They Warrant Effort

Habit 7:
Sharpen the Tongue to Use on Customers and Coworkers

Ponder & Progress:
The Peace of Mind 10

1. How do you, your organization, your leadership, guidance, strategy, communication style, your organization's mission & vision, products and services offer others peace of mind?

2. What peace of mind is to be gained from working with you and for you?

3. How can you and your organization be better positioned as Agents of Peace of Mind in the minds of those you to intend to lead and inspire to action?

4. Do customers, clients, and guests take comfort or feel at ease knowing that you and your organization are on the case? How so?

5. How is working toward your goals bringing you and your team peace of mind?

6. How will accomplishing the goals you are committed to going to bring you and your team peace of mind?

7. How can you help those you lead feel more peace of mind in their work – and in their working relationship with you?

8. What aspects of employee engagement and morale would be improved if all felt more peace at work?

9. How is your organizational culture a catalyst for others to feel peace of mind?

10. How do you offer the Promise of Peace of Mind?

What about Pride and Purpose?

I considered whether I should add Pride *and, to a lesser degree,* Purpose to the Ps of Progress, and decided not to. Over the years, I have asked many friends and peers to describe *feeling pride,* and each has described a special combination of pleasure, peace of mind, and prestige –sometimes with a little pain avoidance, profit, and power thrown into the mix.

Pride may be a solid and realistic sense of one's dignity, value, and self-respect, but the word *pride* is also associated with feeling lofty, or making an arrogant assumption of superiority. *Pride* often has negative connotations, such as haughtiness, vanity, conceit, egoism, grandiosity, narcissism, being a braggart, and so on.

> **"Pride is pleasure arising from a man's thinking too highly of himself."**
> — *Baruch Spinoza*

Excessive pride, according to the writings of Aristotle, is commonly the defining trait that leads to a hero's tragic downfall. Heck, pride is one of the Seven Deadly Sins! Pride is even commonly considered the original and most serious of the deadly sins – the source from which all others arise.

In the story of Lucifer, pride was what caused his fall from heaven, and his transformation into Satan. This story alone shows that *Pride* can be a real downer. So, given its unhappy history, I felt it best that *Pride* not be included as one of the *Ps of Progress.*

At the same time, the rightful feeling of pride –
as in self-respect, or pride in one's work or the work
of the team – is vital for progress.

When people have little or no self-respect or pride
in themselves or their work, they feel increasingly
discouraged, powerless, and inferior.

So, pride is tricky. Speaking of the inflated and
distorted kind of pride, nineteenth-century author
John Ruskin observed: *"In general, pride is at the
bottom of all great mistakes."*

 A Hebrew proverb further admonishes: *"Pride goes
before a fall"* – whether it's a dethroned monarch or
the demoted John Q. Blowhard.

The term *purpose* generally holds different meanings
for different people, but purpose is not a feeling.
Purpose is the idea, the objective, the passion behind
our actions. Our life's purpose is the core compelling
force that pulls us forward.

Purpose is direction with *meaning*.

We develop our meaning based upon what we
believe will result in us feeling the *Six Ps of Progress*.
Having a sense of purpose leads to our feeling the
Six Ps of Progress.

*How do you feel when you know and are following
your purpose?*

When is pride a negative for you?

The Seven Deadly Sins, Visited or Revisited:

These failings, for anyone keeping score, are:
Lust, Gluttony, Greed, Sloth, Wrath, Envy, and Pride.

I sure wish I could share some personal examples of each sin but, to the best of my knowledge – or should I say memory – I have never personally committed any of them. (Stop laughing.)

The idea of Seven Deadly Sins was originally used by early Christian leaders to spotlight – and make people wary of – their tendency to sin. Around the 14th century, the Seven Deadly Sins became a popular theme among artists in Europe.

This helped ingrain them in mass consciousness and culture. Fortunately, each of the deadly sins has an opposite, corresponding virtue, The Seven Holy Virtues. These are: **_Chastity, Abstinence, Liberality, Diligence, Patience, Kindness, and Humility._**

To Thy
Progress Agent
Self Be True

"Step with care and great tact and remember that Life's a Great Balancing Act."
— *Dr. Seuss*

To Thy Progress Agent
Self Be True

Progress Leadership often requires new processes, heightened performance, and traveling untrodden paths. It is tough and more than a tad scary to let go of the familiar and the sense of security that familiarity provides. I have had innumerable conversations with a broad range of committed leaders about how they, or others they know, feel overworked and overwhelmed (not to mention underappreciated and underpaid) in this ever-changing world we live in.

Solid, proactive leaders share with me monthly, if not weekly, how they have "no time" to get it "all" done, and have too many demands placed on them.

Our ideal "stress-free," "healthy," or "right" work-life shifts on a daily basis, and certainly over time. The right balance for us tomorrow will probably be different from what it is for us today. If we want to lead progress we must begin to internalize our motives, the reasons for our actions.

Truly understanding and digging into why we're choosing to do the things we're doing is vital if we're going to lead progress. As humans, we have this dangerous and unavailing habit of always looking at the greener grass on the other side of the fence, unaware that it's really all about our priorities and how we roll out our choices, thoughts, and actions. Leading our own personal progress is a unique jigsaw puzzle, and one in which only we can put together the pieces.

This puzzle is made up of ourselves, our work, our career, our family, our friends, our interests and hobbies, and, in all of the above, our ideals and aspirations. I am not saying that comparing ourselves to others is unnatural.

I am saying that it is not healthy, productive, or even logical. **All we end up doing is comparing our insides with others' outsides.** We compare the way we feel about our lives today *(insides)* to the way other people appear to live: career, house, car, family, friends *(outsides)*. This is not fair to either party. We do not know what is going on in the other person's life or head.

It's like that commercial where the guy has the big house, pool, manicured lawn – the perfect life. He turns to the camera while cruising around his big front yard on his big riding lawn mower and says sadly, *"I am in debt up to my eyeballs."*

As progress agents, we must **Stop measuring ourselves with someone else's yardstick**. Humans love to compete: richer, better-looking, wiser, best-behaved kids, happiest pets, who gets the latest techno-gadget earliest, who understands text-messaging lingo the best. Most of this competition is just wasted effort. In the end, personal progress is a contest with one player – ourselves. The only person we are truly competing against is our current self.

> **"Winning isn't getting ahead of others. It's getting ahead of yourself."**
> — *Roger Staubach*

Sure, it is natural to compete. None of us wants to look or feel like we're lagging behind. So, if we must compete, let's have our contest be about who smiles (with reason) the most, or who is reaching his or her goals and leading progress without stressing. Let's try that. But regardless of their relative merit, and exempting many sports endeavors, most competition appears to be, in essence, foolish, insignificant, absurd, and misguided.

Often, when we are out of *balance*, it is because we're not listening to ourselves. Instead, we're listening to all these other people and their pronouncements about what balance *should* look like. I can't tell you what healthy balance should look like, but I can tell you what it should *feel* like. It should feel like your own nice unique blend of pleasure, prestige, pain avoidance, power, profit and peace of mind.

One of the main things that gets us out of balance is having too much *stuff*. And I don't mean this just in a physical sense; I also mean in our minds and in our pursuits. It is easy to get scattered, and our world is certainly not trying to help us simplify.

For one thing, the sheer volume of information available to us is increasing exponentially. In the 1,500 years between Christ and da Vinci, we had one doubling. Now information doubles every eighteen months.

We must decide and focus on what "in-put" we will put in and act upon – what is most important to us and to the well-being of the people we care about.

If we are going to lead progress in this ever-changing world, it is vital that we invest the bulk of our time and energy in the activities and goals that offer the highest return on the investment for our lives. We cannot do and have 'it all.' We can't know everything there is to know or do everything there is to do. We can't watch every movie, eat at every restaurant, travel to every country, or own every electronic gadget. *Again, there is no way we can do and have 'it all.'* **We have to make choices.**

We've all heard the saying, "the trappings of success." *How about the trappings of **excess**?* Our society wants us to want, and needs us to need stuff, but there is a good chance that we don't need or even want a lot of what we already have. *Time for a garage sale?*

Each of us has a mind; we just have to make it up. To become the type of leader that can lead progress in an ever-changing world, we've got to take the hard, uncompromising look inside ourselves to decide what progress means to us and then continually better ourselves.

> **"The most dangerous leadership myth is that leaders are born-that there is a genetic factor to leadership. That's nonsense; in fact, the opposite is true. Leaders are made rather than born."**
> — *Warren Bennis*

We **_can_** have and do everything we want *if* we truly **_internalize why_** we want it.

Internalize means to make part of one's own individual thinking and being.

Why is the purpose and reasons – meaning the Six Ps of Progress. Passion, desire, and motives for action all come from *internalizing why.* Internalizing takes time, effort, and imagination.

We are each unique, with unique lives and unique priorities. There are so many external influences, such as the media, relatives, neighbors, and coworkers, that get in the way of internalizing the whys for our wants. Internalizing helps us become more deliberate in how we choose to react to events, thoughts, images, emotions, etc.

Successful Progress Leadership, first and foremost, comes down to how we roll within ourselves. It is not someone telling us how we *should* invest our time. Neither life nor business is *"one-size-fits-all."* Progress proceeds from the way we have various options and opportunities sized up in our brain. If we have them positioned and prioritized in a way that helps us - and those we lead - *feel* the right mix of the *Six Ps of Progress*, then we are leading progress. If we don't, we're not. *Simple, but true.*

It would be so easy if we could read a book wherein the author tells us exactly what a healthy progress is for us, and exactly how we should invest our time.

"Step with care and great tact and remember that Life's a Great Balancing Act."
— *Dr. Seuss*

Do I know how you should invest your time? No.
I don't presume to know how you and your team should
invest time. I do not know your goals or what progress
means to you or your organization. *Do you?*

Let's talk big picture… **Life is choices.** We each must
master the choice challenge. We must choose the life
we want from all of life's possibilities. If we don't, we
run the risk of pursuing goals, buying things, and
investing our time the way our boss, significant other,
parents, children, neighbors, and advertisers think is
best – for them. We've all heard tales of industrialist
dads, pushing their artist children to follow in their
footsteps. Certainly, what we choose to do should
benefit others, but has to mean progress for us, too.

People are attempting to persuade us all the time –
to sell us on their ideas – *their* goals for *our* lives!
But it's not really a choice of being sold or not being
sold. It's simply a choice of whom you are going to
be sold by, either yourself or the outside world.

> **"Problems arise in that you have to find
> a balance between what people need from you
> and what you need for yourself."**
> — *Jessye Norman*

It's not that the suggestions that others offer are *"bad"*
ways for us to invest our time. A major challenge to
progressing in life is that we've got a whole bunch of
super-attractive things we can choose to do. For better
or worse, life in this age is a smorgasbord, an *all-you-
can-live buffet of yummy choices*. Not all the choices
on life's smorgasbord are right for us, however, and
not all are healthy, or filling.

110

Imagine you're at a wedding reception. You are about to sit down, and you see a massive buffet table spread out across the back wall of the reception hall.

The buffet has everything from roast beef to lobster, from imported Spanish ham to poached salmon, from artichokes to zucchini. You consider getting yourself some grub before you sit down, but some guy at the table says, *"No, no. Sit down. I'll be happy to get you something."* So you sit.

This dude comes back and sets a big plate of food in front of you. You look down and it's got cottage cheese, gray coleslaw, two elderly cherry tomatoes, some kind of green quiche-looking thing, runny red Jell-O, and about half a pound of pickled okra. Talk about an unbalanced plate.

You think, *"I don't want any of this stuff! I wanted some of the prime rib and smoked salmon!"*

So, now you have some choices.
You may:
A. Eat or pick disgustedly at what has been selected for you.
B. Sit there and go hungry.
C. Get up and fix your own plate.

If we don't choose, we lose. So much of what is out there in the world is irrelevant to what we want to achieve in our lives. Unless we have a true concept of who we are and what we want from the smorgasbord of life, someone will be only too happy to fix a plate for us.

And the plate they fix will consist of what they want us to have based on their own reasons, their whys. We're the only ones who can fix our plate our way.

Each of us has the need and the power, and hears the personal imperative, to craft our own goals and to utilize our resources (time, money, networks, knowledge) to make them happen.

Life is a smorgasbord, so fix yourself a balanced plate – and dig in!

**"Life is like riding a bicycle.
To keep your balance you must keep moving."**
— *Albert Einstein*

We often want to skip the period of transition and quickly get to the other side in order to regain some level of comfort. When dealing with uncertainty, we should be careful not to move too quickly and miss the opportunity to move forward.

Try these proven **Stop, BOP & Roll** strategies for staying motivated, confident and committed to leading progress in an ever-changing world.

To thy Progress Agent self be true.

Be Progress.

Stop

Stop Beating Yourself (and Others) Up.

We are not perfect – *and wouldn't we feel out of place if we were?* Many of us harbor perfectionist standards for ourselves (as well as for others) that are simply unhealthy and unrealistic. *Not good.*

> **"Never discourage anyone... who continually makes progress, no matter how slow."**
> — *Plato* (That "anyone" includes you!)

When we focus on beating ourselves up, we are tearing down our level of resolve and persistence. Believe me, there are plenty of people out there who are only too willing to do that for us. Cut yourself (and others) some slack. _We do not have to be perfect to be progress._

Stop Blaming Others and Holding on to the Past.

It is natural to have difficulty accepting and adjusting to change and uncertainty, especially changes we didn't initiate or think we wanted. Put issues into perspective by focusing on the big picture. Don't focus on the injustice. Focus on your next proactive step.

If we are not careful, we can waste an enormous amount of quality time and energy dwelling on, resenting, and second-guessing the actions of others. This type of thinking can stifle our creativity and our imagination. We get stuck. It is weird to consider, but we can even get comfortable being stuck, because shifting our thoughts is often perceived as being more painful.

113

It helps to begin recognizing the events that don't truly have much effect on our lives and letting them go without getting down on ourselves about letting them go. I am not saying that events don't have consequences, but letting stress and self-doubt impede our progress does not have to be one of them. Things have changed before. Things have progressed before. The only past we should hold onto are the reminders of *past progress.*

Where is your next step forward? Believe you should take it and take it. Don't doubt yourself.
Make something good happen.

Stop Procrastinating!

It doesn't matter how skilled we are or how determined we say we are if procrastination keeps us from getting rolling. Here are the ABC's of why we procrastinate.

A. **We are not truly 100% committed.** We really can't say, *"I am committed; I just haven't done anything yet."* When we're truly committed – WE ACT.

B. **We fear failure.** Ralph Waldo Emerson knew the way around this universal challenge, but most of all he knew the way *through* it: *"Do the thing you fear, and the death of fear is certain."* Action helps remove fear and doubt.

C. **We don't know enough to do the task.** If we don't know how to do something, we have to find out. There are countless ways (books, programs, co-workers, clergy, the Internet) to find reliable info on solid next steps.

<u>Stop</u> Letting Feelings of the Moment get in the Way. There is often a big gap between what we *want* to do and what we *feel* like doing. What we want to do is based on anticipated consequences and educated guesses as to what feelings will be reached. What we *feel* like doing is based on how we *feel* at the moment (tricky). Here is the real kicker: We work best when these are aligned.

Muhammad Ali, arguably the greatest boxer who ever lived, is quoted as saying, *"I hated every minute of the training, but I said, 'Don't quit. Suffer now and live the rest of your life as a champion.'"* He didn't say he didn't *want* to train. He said he *hated* to train. He trained despite his feelings about training. Ali wanted to train because of the benefits of the results he would achieve. He *wanted* to do something he didn't feel like doing because of the progress he would feel. He didn't feel like training but he trained anyway because of outcomes he looked forward to in the future. We mustn't let what we feel like doing hold us back from our progress.

Sometimes we're going to have to vacuum the house, make the outbound calls, pump the iron, skip the desserts, set the alarm, or numerous other acts of will that are not super fun in the moment. But feelings can change quickly. It is vital to base our actions on feelings we aspire to enjoy in the future, and not only on what we feel like doing in a particular moment *(tough to do, but essential).*

> **"Life has a habit of not standing hitched.**
> **You got to ride it like you find it."**
> — *Woody Guthrie*

<u>Stop</u> Stressing and Start Progressing

Over the years I've been surprised by the number
of professionals in my boot camps and in one-on-one
coaching who have shared with me their sense of
being overwhelmed, underappreciated, and underpaid.
Workplace stress is rarely part of anyone's job
description, but it is unfortunately part of most jobs.
It is tough to progress when we are stressed.
In fact, we *feel* stress when we *feel* we are
being *hindered from leading progressing.*

> **"The quality of a leader is reflected in the
> standards they set for themselves."**
> — *Ray Kroc*

Finding healthy and productive ways for Progress
Agents to deal with or relate to the stressful stimuli
in this high-tech, low-touch world of speed-of-light
change is a vital and important topic that desperately
needs discussion. Check this: **Stress not only limits
your progress; stress can and will kill you
(if you don't take action)!**

— The American Medical Association says that
stress is now the basic cause of over 60% of all
diseases and illnesses (cancer, heart problems, etc.).

— Stress-related problems, according to the
American Institute for Stress, are responsible for 75 %
to 90 % of doctor visits.

— A study conducted by the University of
London found that *unmanaged reactions* to stress were
more likely to lead to cancer and heart disease
than either smoking cigarettes or eating foods high
in the bad kind of cholesterol.

Virtually no part of the body escapes the ravages of prolonged negative stress. Unfortunately, many of us make up our minds to "get serious" about our physical and mental health only when we become ill, suffer a heart attack, or experience some other form of breakdown.

Stress is very dangerous, not to mention expensive. Businesses across the USA lose $200-$300 billion dollars annually to stress, resulting in loss in productivity (i.e., less progress) and treatment costs. Effects of stress in the workplace include absenteeism, disruptive outbursts, and the tendency to do as little as possible to get by. All reduce productivity and damage an organization's bottom line. Plus, many of us do not have a well-defined boundary between work and home, and end up taking work problems home with us and letting them affect our personal life.

> **"If you are distressed by anything external, the pain is not due to the thing itself, but to your estimate of it; and this you have the power to revoke at any moment."**
> — *Marcus Aurelius*

I don't mean to stress you out about stress, but the crazy thing to consider is that WE are truly the ultimate *cause* of our own stress. It is our reaction to stressful stimuli that "makes us sick," not the stimuli themselves. We internalize too much outside pressure, which causes inside pressures. No matter what the circumstance, we still have power over the attitude we take toward it. When we feel stress, we become focused on the pain and not the opportunities to take positive steps.

Often, we invest so much time dealing with stress that we don't take time to progress.

We all relate to stimuli differently. What really freaks one person out may excite another, or only mildly irritate a third person. The key is to know in advance positive ways to respond to stressful stimuli.

When our negative reactions to the little stuff build up, it undermines our ability to progress. We become irritable and worn out, which leads to more stress. This is an inappropriate triggering of a very useful survival mechanism. When we're in fight-or-flight mode, we NEED to focus on negatives *(no time to smell the flowers when we're running from a burning building).* But when the same physiological reaction is in response to social situations, we only see the negatives, and lose sight of our strengths, resources and possible action steps.

We often think of stressful stimuli as the big life stuff – like a challenging relationship or a scary economic climate. But a great deal of our anxiety comes from the little day-to-day pressures commonly faced in today's workplace. This dear old world is full of possible "stressors":
- Dissatisfied customers and indecisive prospects
- Our kids, our coworkers, our coworkers' kids
- Technology challenges and industry shifts
- Unrealistic workloads and deadlines
- Slow computers, slow microwaves
- Office gossip and competition
- Long unorganized meetings
- Long commutes in traffic
- Dictatorial leadership

118

These are but a few of the world's never-ending supply of stimuli that we may choose to freak out over, or calmly face.

Our power lies in never losing sight of the fact that it's our _choice_ to get stressed by something or not get stressed by something. We have the choice to be happy, to be mad, to be stressed, to be giddy. _I like giddy._ Nothing can MAKE us stressed, just like, despite the suggestion of many a love song, we can't MAKE someone happy, or vice versa. We can do things we think will encourage them to choose to be happy, but we can not MAKE someone happy. It is their choice. To be stressed is ours. When we are stressed, we are choosing to respond to stimuli in a stressful way. Stress may be normal, but is not necessary.

You control you.
You only control you.
Only you control you.
You control you only.

It feels great to give 110% at work, but it's important to always remember that taking good care of ourselves pays off professionally as well as emotionally. Develop stress immunity and resilience. Invest time in doing what helps you renew your energy. If we are going to put ourselves in the best possible position to lead progress in this ever-changing world, it is vital that we take back control of our lives and careers by _choosing_ to gain control of our thought processes.

Pretending that the stress stimuli are not all around us only increases the problem. The way to lead progress in an ever-changing world is through recognition and action.

"When we commit to action, to actually doing something rather than feeling trapped by events, the stress in our life becomes manageable."
— *Greg Anderson*

Ponder & Progress:
Too Stressed to Progress?

1. When do you feel overworked and overwhelmed?
2. What are you allowing yourself to get stressed about?
3. What physical challenges are you having that may be related to stress?
4. Do you have trouble sleeping due to stress?
5. Is it time to get serious about your stress?
6. How can you be better prepared for stressful stimuli?
7. How can you choose not to stress?
8. Do you have too many demands on your time?
9. Are you too stressed to progress?
10. Can you DO something about a stressful situation?
Bet you CAN, and if you can ...DO IT.

"Stress is the trash of modern life – we all generate it but if you don't dispose of it properly, it will pile up and overtake your life."
— *Danzae Pace*

B.O.P. – Be Open to Progress

Our mind-set is the first thing we have to empower if we're going to lead progress in an ever-changing world. This is especially true in this ever-changing, always challenging marketplace. While any number of actions and initiatives may be employed to progress, our minds must first be willing. Often, when the going gets tough, the mind has to get tough to get going.

It may be uncomfortable and even painful, but we must *shift our focus to the possible* if we are to harness our potential. Each of has unbelievable potential, which, for the most part, is only limited by our minds. It takes guts to confront an uncertain future. But that future, though unpredictable, also brings the possibility of progress.

> **"When you hit a wrong note, it's the next note you play that determines if it's good or bad."**
> — *Miles Davis*

Even unwanted "change" can present opportunities, but we've got to be in the right mental state to identify and pounce on them. Turbulence and problems are life forces that may be seen as opportunities for growth and advancement. Be open to change as an opportunity to progress.

Acceptance evokes our personal power to navigate change and lead progress. Some transitions are welcomed and some are not. Either way, recognize that we are engaged in a transition, and our attention is needed.

In bop music of the 1940s, musical interaction between the soloist and the drummer was referred to as "dropping bombs." When the world "drops bombs" and sends its jazzy licks our way, we need to feel we have bombs to drop as well that will put us back in the groove (or at least know where we can find shelter).

Be ready, willing, and able to improvise. We create our future with our responses to change. Interact with the change, get intimate with it. We cannot control what happens to us, but we can control our reaction to what happens to us. When we open up to new experiences, we discover potential in ourselves we never knew we had. Often, it takes more effort not to do something than to do it. It helps to be flexible in how we view problems. We need to quit burning up our energy shooting down ideas. Latch on to a couple of ideas and go for it. Think *"I'll try that"* instead of *"That won't work."*

"Dwell in possibility." — *Emily Dickinson*

Invent your future by committing to lifelong learning. Knowing that change is coming and even why we must change is not enough; it helps to know how to progress. Be ready for the world and its endless opportunities for progress. Learn what you need to learn, and more.

Action steps often need time to work. It's important to give them that time. However, we must also be open-minded enough to know when to use alternate approaches and strategies to move forward. Commit to progress, not to a plan. Commit to action. Keep your eyes, ears, mind, and heart open for ways to lead progress in an ever-changing world.

Be Open to Progress: Ten Tips

1. Make Some YOU Time.

YOU time is not a luxury. YOU time is not wasted time.
We all need to turn it down a bit from time to time.
YOU time is vital to your progress. Invest time in
relaxing.   The key is the mental break. Don't even
think about feeling guilty about this YOU time.
Fun and leisure are vital for recharging our lives.

- Read a book or magazine *(the one you just haven't had time to read).*
- Watch your favorite childhood movie.
- Have coffee with a friend.
- Visit a museum or library.
- Take a power nap.
- Listen to your soothing, relaxing music.
- Get a hobby.
- Stretch; maybe try Pilates or yoga.
- Meditate.
- Garden.
- Take a hot shower or warm bath.
- Get a massage. *Maybe you have the need to be kneaded.*
- Take a vacation; even a 20-minute one can help.

Important Note: Vacations should be vacations.
It's not a vacation if you're reading business emails
and taking a bunch of business calls.

**"It isn't the past which holds us back,
it's the future; and how we undermine it, today."**
— Dr. Viktor Frankl

2. Think Lovely Thoughts. *

Yes, I am talking about affirmations. We use affirmations all the time; it's just that most of them are negative, stress-inducing, and self-limiting.

> *"My job stinks."*
> *"I am stressed out."*
> *"I can't catch a break."*

Our brains are trippy and complicated, and can do amazing things. But at their core, our brains want one thing: **To Be Right.** Whatever we continually tell ourselves about ourselves and our lives, our brains are working overtime to make true.

> **"You gotta fight, fight, fight for your mind,**
> **while you got the time."**
> — *Ben Harper*

Visualize the good. Optimism is an asset. Practice self-talk that emphasizes a self-affirming attitude. Stuff like:

"Things work out for me."   *"This is good day."*
"I make good decisions."   *"This is a great book."*

Worry is a poor use of imagination. It is imperative that we be careful about the things we say to ourselves, and to talk to ourselves as a winner to a winner. As I mentioned earlier, *your brain is a terrible thing to use against yourself.*

*__*Think Lovely Thoughts__ is what Peter Pan told John, Michael, and Wendy they would have to do to learn to fly in the song, "I'm Flying." Peter also blew fairy dust on them but I don't know where you can get your hands on any of that. The kids came up with lovely thoughts like: Fishing, Hoopskirt, Candy, Picnics, Summer, More Candy, Sailing, Flowers, still more Candy, and Christmas.*

3. Say YES to NO.

It is common for leaders to take on too many responsibilities. Being too busy is a big source of stress in today's *get, get & go, go, go* world. We are so chronically over-scheduled that we never give ourselves a chance to offer our best in the moment.

> **"You can only do so much.
> There are five more projects you want to do,
> but you pick the three that are really going to
> matter, and you try to do those really well,
> and you don't even try to do the others."**
> — *Sheryl Sandberg*

It is possible that we could get more done by doing less. When we internalize the difference between *full* and *fulfilling*, we realize it's not how many events we attend or projects we oversee that's important. We do not have to say "yes" to every demand on our time. And we shouldn't feel bad, since we are saying "no" to the event or project, not the person.

Progress Agents must internalize that being busy can wear us out. If we are committed to leading progress in this ever-changing world, we must know our limits and not limit our NOs.

— Simplify – get rid of the clutter in your office and in your life.

— Review priorities and see if a request fits. When you see things that hinders your ability to lead progress, speak up.

— Stop trying to make everyone happy. (We can't do it anyway.) A polite way to say NO to a request for YOUR time: *"I'm quite committed. I can be your backup, but please keep searching."*

4. Air In. Air Out.

Deep breathing is one of the best stress-relief methods, often recommended but rarely utilized. Deep breathing works as long as you don't do it right in front of your boss or a customer. Here is the classic method in a four-step process:

Step 1: *Close your eyes and focus only on breathing.* *

Step 2: *Take a long breath in.*

Step 3: *Hold for three to five seconds.*

Step 4: *Slowly exhale.*

Repeat five to 10 times, as needed. Whether you breathe in through the nose and/or out through the mouth, is irrelevant. It is the deep abdominal breathing that's inherently relaxing.

* Do keep eyes open if driving or playing racquetball.

5. Break a Sweat and Let Off Some Steam.

Have you heard about this new craze? They call it…regular exercise! When our lives seem to be up in the air, exercise can keep us grounded. Exercise releases mood-enhancing, feel-good chemicals like endorphins, the mind-body's natural painkiller and mood-calmer. We feel better when we get a good workout in. Plus, exercise gives us a positive sense of accomplishment – and our clothes don't fit as tightly.

It is recommended that we shoot for 30 minutes of some good sweaty physical activity three to four times a week. But even five minutes here and there throughout the day is going to make a difference in how we view stressful stimuli.

Even brisk walking and light stretching feel good and can help you stay in control. Be your own bouncer and take it outside. Fresh air and natural full-spectrum light add checks to the "*Good for You*" column. The main thing is to find ways of exercising that are fun for you. *Find exercise lonely or boring?* Get a friend to break a sweat with you. I bet they could use the exercise and the endorphins just as much as you.

6. Budget Your Spending, and Save, Save, Save.
We all know that debt is a big, big problem. Statistics on American household debt are astounding. Living in the shadow of mountainous debt leaves little room for light or air. Its presence, always lumbering overhead and ever on our mind, means constant stress. And if we should momentarily forget about it, the phone is sure to ring at dinnertime with a friendly reminder from the Bank of Interruptions.

To lead progress in an ever-changing world, we must be willing to alter our spending behavior so we can sleep nights and get to where we want to be.

- Establish financial goals. **Commit** to achieving them.
- Pay off your whole credit card bill each month.
- Don't wait to start saving. Time is ticking.
- Get enough life insurance.
- Do not let emotions drive buying or investment decisions.

> **"If you would be wealthy, think of saving as well as getting."**
> — *Benjamin Franklin*

7. Sleep Tight and Right.

A fresh mind and body are better able to relate powerfully to stressful stimuli. Let there be no doubt: Our minds and bodies need down-time for rejuvenation.

Get seven to eight hours of sleep every night. *Yeah, I know – seven to eight every night is tough.* At least go to bed at the same time each night. Give your mind and body the rest needed to recharge.

It is common when we are stressed to have difficulty in falling asleep, even if we have made it to bed at a good hour. This really stinks, because the stress has already worn us out and now we can't nod off, which makes us even more stressed, tired, irritable, and unable to lead progress.

When having trouble falling asleep, take a warm shower or bath and try not to focus on the effects of *not* sleeping because that will just keep you from sleeping.

You might even consider trying Dr. Viktor Frankl's technique of paradoxical intent. That is, if all else fails, pretend that you must stay awake, or convince yourself that staying awake is a good thing, that nothing bad will come of it, and that it will give you a great opportunity to let your mind wander.

Putting a jolly spin on sleeplessness, even if it at first feels phony, will at least calm you down, and may even work in the way that Dr. Frankl envisioned.

8. Give Mind and Body the "Right Fuel."

Challenges take energy.   A lack of the "right fuel" can cause a bunch of problems like fatigue, lack of concentration, low morale, halitosis, death-by-Twinkies, etc. Our minds and bodies respond more effectively to stressful stimuli when they are getting the right nutrients.

Give your body the right fuel for life's challenges. As Jean Anthelme Brillat-Savarin wrote, *"Tell me what you eat, I'll tell you who you are."*

Hey, I'm not the guru on nutrition, and you don't need one anyway. You know what the "Right Fuel" is. It's the stuff we try to make kids eat. *As for drinking alcohol: Hangovers never add to the bottom line.*

9. Become Flexible in Problem Solving.

Allow yourself the time to work through challenges and find the best, possibly new or unique, way to lead progress. Be willing to try new solutions.

Long commutes and driving in heavy traffic can seem like a big waste of time. Have mind-expanding podcasts to listen to. Rigid thinking encourages stress.

- Don't let assumptions limit possible solutions.
- Chop up big problems and challenges into smaller ones. Address each component individually.
- Ask several people for their advice and suggestions.
- Alter your point of view. Imagine yourself as a child, a billionaire, or even riding on a beam of light*.

*__*Beam me up Einstein*__:*
It is said that Albert Einstein imagined riding on a beam of light when he came up with his theory of relativity. Pretty good theory.

Important Note:
If you feel like your stress is just too much, talk with your family, a friend, or a counselor.
Ask for help. Talk it out.

The strong get help.
Do not let stress impede your ability to lead progress in an ever-changing world.

> **"Stress and worry, they solve nothing.
> What they do is block creativity.
> You are not even able to
> think about the solutions.
> Every problem has a solution."**
> — *Susan L. Taylor*

10. Find the Humor.
As legendary director Mel Brooks said,
"Humor is just another defense against the universe."
Our minds can only focus on one thing at a time.
When we find the humor in a situation, it automatically relieves stress because the humor takes the place of stress, washing it away in waves of laughter and sometimes even rivers of tears.
Laughter is good medicine.

Humor is a learned coping skill that improves with practice. When we laugh, similar to when we exercise, endorphins are released in the brain that help us feel better about the situation and offer more energy to tackle challenges.

> **"Humor was another of the soul's weapons
> in the fight for self-preservation."**
> — *Dr. Viktor Frankl*

130

"Belly laughs" are also said to give our innards
a good workout, massaging our organs while
warming our hearts. *Touching, isn't it?*

**"I'm happy that I have brought laughter because
I have been shown by many the value of it
in so many lives, in so many ways."**
— Lucille Ball

Humor also happens to be profitable.
People are drawn to people who are upbeat and
have a positive, jovial frame of mind. Professionals
who maintain a sense of humor gain respect.

**"The attempt to develop a sense of humor and to
see things in a humorous light is some kind of a
trick learned while mastering the art of living."**
— Dr. Viktor Frankl

Find what makes you laugh. And be sure to laugh
at yourself from time to time.

Consider…
What makes you laugh?
Where is the humor in the situation?

**"There are three things that are real –
God, human folly, and laughter.
The first two are beyond comprehension.
So we must do what we can with the third."**
— John F. Kennedy

Dropping Bombs on Bop

World War II played a big role in bringing about bop music. The war after "The War to End All Wars" drafted many of the established musicians of the day to play in the armed forces' big bands. Younger musicians, like Dizzy Gillespie, Charlie Parker, and Thelonious Monk (many teenagers, and too young to be drafted), were left to play in clubs and touring bands.

Financial cutbacks and an entertainment tax (both brought on by the war effort) encouraged these young musicians to make do with less. In streamlining their bands to four to six musicians, they'd unwittingly created a perfect vehicle for exploring the improvisational elements of jazz and blues music.

Freed from the demands and constraints of the Big Band arrangements, these smaller bebop groups allowed for a flowing improvisation among all the musicians. Bop became a new direction for jazz, and a new art form unto itself.

Rhythmically in bop music, the steady beat is assigned to the bass player and the ride and hi-hat cymbals of the drummer. This new approach allowed drummers (like Max Roach) to interact with the soloist, creating rhythmic accents with the bass drum and snare, almost like a shifting call and response. This interaction in bop music was referred to as "dropping bombs."

Jamming musically is not so different from improvisation with, and attunement to, the situations and people we interact with every day. All of us can BOP our way to progressive rhythms in our own lives.

132

Roll

Make action the way you roll. As Will Rogers said, *"Even if you are on the right track, you'll get run over if you just sit there."* Consistently be doing something you believe will help you lead progress.

Start now. Take some action. Be dynamic. Dare to fail. Time is ticking. The sooner you find out what doesn't work, the sooner you will find out what will. And the sooner you start, the sooner you will lead progress. With each small step you grow in confidence.

Think of some action that you could take that you believe would help you and your team advance by even a baby-step toward your goal. Take that step.

Progress is a step forward. Help your team take today's step. Take risks. Give it your best shot.

Focus on NOW rather than later. Today is all we have, so make the most of it. *Got a new idea, a way to tweak an existing sales practice, customer-service initiatives, or a step you could take toward your goals?* The best time to do anything about it is N-O-W.

Focus on what you are doing today to move your organization toward the goal, rather than thinking, *"I have to wait for this thing or that thing to happen first."*

Note: There will always be reasons for **NOT** taking action. Procrastinators can find every reason under the sun. Encourage your team not to wait for that one big thing to happen before taking action and moving forward. Don't wait for the right mood to strike.

Do one small thing today that you believe will help you lead progress, no matter how small. The point is to start immediately. Stop reading this and go do it – *but then please come back!*

Develop the *Do it now* habit. Be assertive. Be proactive. You are most likely on a learning curve, so round that corner.

As Confucius is quoted as saying *"Our greatest glory is not in never falling, but in rising every time we fall."* After assessing the likely consequences, make it okay to fail, to try new things. It's how we grow, wise up, and lead progress in an ever-changing world.

The Progress Agent's Three Step System for Leading Progress

Step 1: Get Reliable Information.
Step 2: Act on Reliable Information.
Step 3: Repeat

That's it. Get reliable information, Act on reliable information, Repeat. If the information turns out not to be useful, *guess what we do?* Get *reliable* information and act on *reliable* information, over and over and over and over.

> **"When any real progress is made, we unlearn and learn anew what we thought we knew before."**
> — *Henry David Thoreau*

Today, information is readily available for the asking. Good info is everywhere – on the Internet, in books, recordings, and seminars. Really, not knowing how to do something is the weakest of excuses. If we want something badly enough, there are ways to get the info we need, even if we have to pay someone for it.

Instead of thinking, *I don't know how,* ask yourself: *Where can I get the new information (read: knowledge and skills) I need?*

Find someone to bounce ideas off of. Form a Progress Leadership Mastermind group. Everyone knows someone who has a talent or skill that can complement their own. Put your minds together to create what you want. Instead of assuming that we are in this alone and that no one can help us, we should continually ask ourselves, *"Who can help me and how can I help them?"*

When change comes *(and it's coming)*, it's up to Progress Agents to relate decisively to that change, rather than passively allowing the change to take us where it may. We have the choice of taking control of our actions and the situations, and leading progress.

We'll never know the outcomes unless we try. We can always revamp and act again. Better to fail from making an effort than from inertia. *Why not try?*

Do the next right thing, or at least do something that you believe is the next right thing. Better to do the right thing wrong, than the wrong thing right. The key is to DO something. Learn something. Try something.

There is always time to lead progress. Time is the great equalizer. Each day, every one of us gets the same amount – 24 hours – 1440 minutes. Nobody gets less. Nobody gets more.

Time can not be slowed, stopped, sped up, or saved like money. Time's ticking, always ticking. **Time Management is really Self-Management, with a respect for time.**

What is an effective use of your time? The answer is totally subjective because the value of the results is subjective. What makes a wise investment of time for me may not be a wise investment for you.

> **"Until we manage time, we can manage nothing else."**
> — *Peter Drucker*

Each of us is, however, investing some of our time in daily activities that do not serve our goals. Too much time is allotted to fleeting interests that we know are less important than progressing toward our crafted goals. That is why it is so important to remind ourselves of the benefits of our goals.

All of us have said to ourselves, *"Oh, I really would like to (fill in the blank), if I could only FIND the time."* Time does not need to be _found_. It is right here. Time needs to be invested wisely. Each day we are _choosing_ to invest our time somewhere, and for a reason. By investing our time more wisely, we minimize stress, improve our quality of life, and have time to focus on leading progress in an ever-changing world.

Ponder & Progress:
Always Time to Lead Progress

1. _When do you feel you waste time?_

2. _Is procrastination a problem?   How so?_

3. _Do you need to exercise better "time management?" Why?_

4. _What are two important things in your life that must be done but aren't?_

5. _What are the most valuable uses of your time right now?_

6. _Do you list and rank tasks that need to be done each day?_

7. _During what part of the day are you most productive or effective?_

8. _What are two actions that you do weekly that could and should be done by someone else?_

9. _What is the best use of your time in terms of your short-term goals?_

10. _What is the best use of your time in terms of your long-term goals?_

Ten Time Tips for Progress Leadership

1. "To Do" or Not "To Do"

In the late 1920s, Charles Schwab, president of the then fledgling Bethlehem Steel Company (unrelated to the discount brokerage of the same name), asked management consultant and efficiency expert Ivy Lee to help him and his team become more productive.

After observing Schwab for several hours, Ivy told him that he could teach a time-management system in about 20 minutes that would enable Schwab and his executives to get 50% more work done, without working harder or longer.

Schwab asked what this advice would cost him. Lee replied, *"Use the plan for six months and send me a check for how much you think it is worth."*

Lee recommended the following:

1. Write down the things you have to do the next day.

2. Number these tasks in the order of their importance.

3. Start your day by working on the first item on your list and stick with it until it's accomplished (or until you've done as much as you can); then go on to the next one, and so on.

Six months later, Lee received a check from Schwab for $25,000, equivalent to $400,000 in today's world. *Four hundred thousand dollars – for a To-Do List tip?* I should have charged more for this book!

138

Charles Schwab and his executives took Ivy's "To-Do List" advice, and within five years turned Bethlehem Steel Company into the biggest steel producer in the world.

A To-Do List is common sense, right?
But is it common practice?

The key is to address the most important thing first, and not to look over the additional fifteen "To-Do" items until Number One is completed. That way, we won't see Number Twelve and say, "*Oh, that won't take very long, so I'll do that first. It's easier.*" Prioritizing ensures that we are investing our time and energy in those tasks and steps that bring the biggest benefits to our lives. *If we don't know what we should be doing, how can we manage our time to do it?*

It is OK, and normal, to have stuff left on your list at the end of the day. If you follow Ivy's system, you have worked on the most important thing already. The other stuff flows through to the next day.

Try this… Devote at least an hour to the most important thing on his To-Do List even before you check your email. Even if you can't get this most important thing done in an hour or so, you are more likely to get back to it quickly because you have gotten it going.

Some folks feel compelled to write out their To-Do List by hand, saying they feel it instills more commitment into each item because they are willing to rewrite it each day until the item gets crossed off.

There's also the thought that the act of physically writing on paper somehow sets the task in cerebral-stone, making it more likely to be accomplished. *Cool. Rock on.*

Other folks prefer to use some form of time-management software that can break their list into manageable chunks. *Again, cool. Rock on.*

Figure out what works for you and don't "make a big to-do" (old idiom for "complain too much") about it. Just do the "To Do."

2. Construct Structure by Planning with a Planner. Most successful Progress Agents have some kind of time-management system – BlackBerry, paper day planner, *something*. Keep it with you at all times, adding to it and striking off completed items, and set aside time for specific tasks like prospecting, networking, and follow-ups.

Setting a specific time period – even a specific place – to make calls significantly increases the chances of actually doing it. Reduce the risk of procrastination, time-frittering, and "puttering" by formalizing tasks. **We don't find time or make it; we schedule time and take it.** When using a planner, be sure to track your goals and your use of time. Solid tracking helps develop a better sense of what we can accomplish in a given period of time.

> **"If you want to make good use of your time, you've got to know what's most important and then give it all you've got."**
> — *Lee Iacocca*

140

3. Set a Realistic Schedule.

It is common to overestimate how much can be done within a given time and try to pack too much into our day. The residues of a crowded day are often frustration, careless errors, disappointment, and even self-punishment. And it is not just we who suffer. The people in our day suffer as well because we are scattered, unprepared, or late for appointments.

"You can and should set your own limits and clearly articulate them. This takes courage, but it is also liberating and empowering, and often earns you new respect."
— *Rosalind Brewer*

Setting realistic schedules gives us a little time to chill. Chilling doesn't mean turning off. Giving ourselves a little breathing room enables us to think things through, regroup, refocus, or maybe come up with new ideas that could positively help us lead progress.

4. Delegate Right.

We can accomplish a lot more with help. We shouldn't just delegate to full-time employees. Delegating can also include others whom we turn to so that we can lead progress in other ways.

Delegation is not dumping. Think of outsourcing as delegating. I outsource my lawn care, bookkeeping, and pizza baking. *(Thanks, Pizza Hut.)*

As leaders, if something we assign doesn't get done right, it is on us. Either WE: A.) did not communicate the task clearly enough, and/or provide the right tools; or we B.) delegated the task to the wrong person.

141

Delegating to *wrong* person with *wrong* information
leads to change.
Delegating to *right* person with *wrong* info information
leads to change.
Delegating to *wrong* person with *right* information
leads to change.
Delegating to *right* person with *right* information
leads to ***progress****.*

The **right** info means providing:
- Clear goals (Objectives must be clear, but allow attendant procedures to vary. Guard against any tendency you may have to micro-manage.)
- Training (online, classroom and/or on the job)
- Realistic deadlines (Make sure those you delegate to know the relative importance of the task.)
- Rewards/Consequences

What are some things you are doing daily that others could do, so that you would have the time to do the things YOU want to do?

"In truth, people can generally make time for what they choose to do; it is not really the time but the will that is lacking."
— *Sir John Lubbock*

5. Focus on Being Effective More Than Being Efficient.
There's a big difference between "effectiveness" and "efficiency." When we are efficient, we are able to carry out tasks in a short time. However, we won't be effective unless those actions result in us moving closer to our personal and/or organizational goals.

Efficiency means producing outcomes quickly.

Effectiveness means producing desired outcomes.

Sometimes, becoming more efficient leads to becoming less effective. For example, in this fast pace of life and business, we naturally seek more efficient ways to communicate. We send e-mails rather than make phone calls, and have phone meetings rather than meeting face-to-face. Although these may appear to be more efficient ways to communicate, they may actually be less effective than the methods they replace.

Clearly, being both effective and efficient should be the aim, but if effectiveness is lost for the sake of efficiency, then the whole purpose for doing whatever it is we're doing is defeated. Sales calls can be made very efficiently, twenty-five an hour. But if sales or appointments are the goal, the calls are not very effective. We can deal with customer issues efficiently, but not necessarily effectively.

Sometimes we are simply doing the wrong things. In his book, *The 4-Hour Workweek,* Timothy Ferriss shares how we shouldn't waste time being efficient in tasks that are not effective, and that we should work to limit or eliminate such time-wasters.

The 80-20 Rule, or Pareto Principle, states that 80 percent of the reward or effect from any endeavor comes from 20 percent of the effort. The trick to being effective is to isolate and identify that valuable 20 percent and put most of your energy into those efforts.

There is definitely a need for efficiency. But efficiency is never the goal. Effectiveness is what is ultimately important, and effectiveness is personal. Nothing vital should be given up for the sake of being efficient. Better to do the right thing wrong, than the wrong thing right. Of course, it is best to do the right things right. One key to a happy, successful life is to look for ways to efficiently be more effective at leading progress.

80+20 words on the Pareto Principle:
Twentieth-century management consultant Joseph M. Juran coined this well-established principle, naming it after Italian economist and philosopher Vilfredo Pareto. Pareto had observed that 80% of his country's wealth was controlled by 20% of its population. Juran, whose teachings focused on managing for quality, expanded Pareto's principle, applying it to productivity issues. (For example, 80% of our sales come from 20% of our customers.) Although the principle is also known as "the vital few and the trivial many," Joseph Juran preferred "the vital few and the useful many" as a way to show that the remaining 80% should not be ignored.

6. Progress Leadership Blocks.
Block out time for important tasks, such as making calls, reading trades, opening mail, taking a nap. (I am not kidding.) Blocking time is especially useful when dealing with email.

Just because someone can contact us immediately via email doesn't mean that we must reply immediately. Most people are not looking for an immediate response, just a timely one. I used to check email every time I'd hear the *Bing!* "You've got mail." Now I turn off the sound. It's simply not an effective investment of time to read and answer each and every email as it arrives.

144

As long as our most important contacts know how to reach us in an emergency, we can schedule email correspondence for four to six times per day.

7. Make a Molehill Out of the Mountain.

JOKE -   *Q: How do you eat an elephant?*
             A: One bite at a time.

Most of the time, starting projects is more challenging than finishing them. We see this big project we'd love to accomplish, we doubt we will ever finish it, so we don't even start. The key to *putting off putting off* is to break projects into manageable chunks, so we are not overwhelmed by them. Start!

> **"He who has begun has half done.**
> **Dare to be wise; begin!"**
> — *Horace*

8. Know Your Progress Leadership Clock.

Try to schedule important activities and tough projects during your period of peak productivity. *When is that?* Everybody is different, but each of us has a time of day (or night) when we tend to be most productive.

To figure out yours, try keeping a *Take Time for Progress* journal for one or two weeks. Record tasks performed and associated time values to uncover time that can be utilized more wisely. Identify time-wasters. We can learn a great deal by monitoring ourselves at 30-minute intervals. At every half hour, consider: *What behaviors must be altered to lead progress?* Design your daily schedule to keep your best time available for YOUR most important projects.

145

9. Find Dots. Make Dots. Connect Dots.
Build More Priceless Business Relationships.
Is this a time-management tip? You bet.
The more priceless business relationships with other Progress Agents we have, the quicker and more efficiently we can uncover opportunities to get things done.

> *For team progress to grow,*
> *Our foe is not the status quo,*
> *But our internal drive to gain access*
> *To people and solutions we do not yet know.*

Get out there, connect and build priceless business relationships!

> ### "Instead of better glasses, your network gives you better eyes."
> — *Ronald Burt*

10. Dare to Take Time.
If we don't have the time to do it right, we don't have time to do it wrong. Doing our work right the first time often takes more time upfront, but correcting a flurry of careless errors usually results in more time spent in the long run. I know it may sound odd, but often good "time management" means responding slower to some tasks. For example, if we are investing time in a high-priority activity, we might not answer the phone while we're doing it. We need to take the time we need to do a quality job.

Stop, B.O.P. and Roll your way to leading progress in an ever-changing world. Commit to Progress Leadership. Be a Progress Agent. *Be Progress.*

Ponder & Progress:
To Thy Progress Agent Self Be True

1. What changes in the past have you transitioned
Into personal progress?

2. What changes are reshaping your industry?

3. What changes are happening in your personal life?

4. How will you lead progress in the change?

5. What do you need to stop doing or thinking
to start progressing?

6. What feelings are you letting get in your way?

7. How can you become more open to progress?

8. What do you need to "unlearn" to progress?

9. Where can you get reliable information?

10. When will you make action the way you roll?

> **"Weep not that the world changes –
> did it keep a stable, changeless state,
> 'twere cause indeed to weep."**
> — _William Cullen Bryant_

The Umbrella Man

Several years ago at 9:45 am on a cold and super rainy Saturday morning, I got in my car and made the seven-and-a-half- minute trip to my local Blockbuster (Remember, Blockbuster? Remember, DVDs?).

I was on a mission to snag, for me and my kids, *Swiss Family Robinson*, an early Disney Classic and a perfect movie for a rainy Saturday.

Blockbuster had not opened yet, so I walked down the sidewalk, checking out the other shops and waiting for 10:00 a.m. when Blockbuster would open. The rain was really coming down, but I stayed dry walking under the shopping center's awning.

About four shops down from Blockbuster, I noticed a small, healthy-looking Korean man who appeared to be about fifty years old. He was standing in front of a little donut shop under the awning.

The man was holding a HUGE blue umbrella and facing the rain. The donut shop was the only place open along this strip of shops, and it was packed with people.

Umbrella Man just stood there, full of life, huge smile on his face. He was in no hurry; in fact, he seemed to be totally content. As I walked past him, we acknowledged each other and said hello.

My curiosity was piqued.
What was this guy up to?

149

I looked around. At first, I thought maybe he was waiting for one of the other shops to open. But if that was true, *why did he still have the big blue umbrella open? Why not just close the big thing and wait?* Plus, his back was to the shops. He was looking out at the parking lot and the rain.

Was he waiting for someone?
Maybe, but he seemed really involved in the moment (big smile, eyes wide).

Maybe he liked to watch the rain.
I do.

Maybe he was waiting for a change in the weather before he headed to his car. *But wasn't that what the big blue umbrella was for?*

Why did he need such a big umbrella, anyway?
Then I remembered a small poster I'd seen on the wall of an organization where I was conducting a Progress Leadership Culture Transformation consulting project. The small poster said:

We cannot promise others sunny weather, but we can promise to hold an umbrella over them when it rains.

Suddenly it hit me. I knew what he was up to.
I spun around and blurted, *"This is your donut shop*!" (If you know me, you know I blurt.)

The man turned to me, smiled, and said proudly, with a thick Korean accent, *"It is, yes."*

"And you are standing here with the umbrella waiting for your customers."

"Yes," he replied with a real upbeat kick in his voice. *"I go out with my umbrella and bring them in. When they are ready to leave, I walk them to their cars."*

I paused, nodded, and said, *"Wow. That's really good customer service!"*

He smiled, shook his head, and said, *"No. It is my pleasure."*

From the look in his eyes and the tone of his voice, I could tell he MEANT it. It was HIS pleasure. He wasn't just holding the umbrella for his customers. He was doing it for himself as well. In this simplest of ways, he was leading progress in an ever-changing world. The change in this case was the rain and the risk of his loyal customers getting wet.

I went back more than a year later to get the Donut Man's name and background for this book, and he remembered our conversation. His name is Inlark Han. He and his wife, Yoon, immigrated to the United States in 2001, along with their children, Jaeyoung and Seongmee, for their children's education. They bought an established donut shop, Sonny Donuts around that same time.

Inlark got the idea for the big blue umbrella after watching customers battle the rain to come into his store. Being in a shopping center, Sonny Donuts does not have a drive-thru.

Inlark knew that when it rains, his customers could easily visit one of the several nearby competitors' drive-thrus to avoid getting wet. To show his appreciation, Inlark went out and bought the big blue umbrella.

Besides baking awesome (read: not oily) donuts and being a top-notch umbrella man, Inlark makes a point of greeting each customer by name when they visit. With her upbeat attitude, lively eyes, and enormous smile, Yoon is a big hit with customers as well.

Neither let their limited English intimidate them. Yoon says, *"We may not speak English well, but we try and we smile. And many customers want to learn some Korean too. That is nice."*

Sonny Donuts is open seven days a week, from 5:00 a.m. until noon. Inlark and Yoon start baking each day at 1:30 a.m. Their busiest day is Saturday, with Sunday a close second.   Customers - including me – rave about their kolaches *(pigs in a blanket to us Southern folk)* because they are light and tasty.

Was Inlark greeting his customers with a huge umbrella when it rains good for business?   Yes.

Think it will help inspire loyal customers?   You bet.

Will holding that umbrella help make his business more successful? Absolutely.

All of the above is obviously good for him and his business, but it's also good for his customers and he found joy in the process.

Greeting his customers with that huge umbrella brought him pleasure *(as well as prestige, pain avoidance, power, profit and peace of mind).* It offered his customers these Six Ps of Progress as well.

The Umbrella/Donut Man wasn't complaining about the change in the weather or waiting for the weather to change; in this simple way he had found a way to Help, to Serve, to Lead Progress in an ever-changing world.

Remember:
Change is Inevitable, Progress is a Choice.

Remember:
All Progress is Change, but not all Change is Progress.

Remember:
Leaders must be viewed as Progress Agents not merely change agents.

Remember:
We Progress as We Help Others Progress.

Remember:
Progress does not Demand Perfection,
only Persistence.

Remember:
Progress is a Step Forward.
Help your Team Take Today's Step.

Commit to Progress Leadership.
Be a Progress Agent.

Be Progress.

About the Author:

Dean Lindsay is the President of The Progress Agents LLC, an education organization dedicated to *Empowering Progress in Sales, Service and Workplace Culture.* He is the Host of *The DEAN's List* on the C-Suite TV Network, and has been hailed as 'America's Progress Agent' by *The Strategic HR Forum* as well as:

- ✓ an *'outstanding thought leader on the subject of building priceless business relationships'* by *Sales and Marketing Executives International,*
- ✓ *'The Dean of Sales and Service'* by *Business Class News,*
- ✓ *'A Master of Progress' by* Jay Conrad Levinson, the legendary Father of *Guerrilla Marketing.*

Dean is a powerful keynote speaker with a humorous and engaging approach. He has had the privilege of sharing his profitable business growth and workplace culture insights in countries across the globe including: *Spain, Turkey, Poland, Ecuador, Mexico, Canada, Venezuela, Sweden and the islands of Aruba and Jamaica.*

Dean's national and international clients include the *United States Patent & Trademark Office, Marriott, Smoothie King, American Airlines, Handheld (Sweden), Texas A&M, New York Life, Aramark Canada, Nestle, Precision Tune Auto Care, American Express, Heinz, Hilton, Pacific Life & Annuity, FASTSIGNS, Western Union, Gold's Gym, EKOS (Ecuador), ConocoPhillips, Haggar Clothing, and the United States Peace Corp.*

Dean is an active member of the *Viktor Frankl Institute of Logotherapy,* a cum laude graduate of the *University of North Texas* and served as Guest Lecturer to *UCLA Anderson School of Management* as well as the *International Customer Management Institute.*

Dean has been a featured contributor to *CEO World Magazine*, *The Smart Manager* (India), *Business Class News, Sales and Service Excellence*, *Training Magazine Europe*, and the American Management Association's *Moving Ahead* magazine. His business views have been featured on *Voice of America* radio and *Monster.com*.

Dean's books have sold over 100,000 copies worldwide and have been translated into *Chinese, Hindi, Polish, Korean, Spanish and Greek.*

Dean, his wife Lena, and their two smart, strong, and beautiful daughters, Sofia & Ella, live in Texas.

<u>*Endorsements for Dean Lindsay as Keynote Speaker:*</u>

"If you want a standing ovation from your audience, have Dean as your speaker. He got one from our company."
                    — *John Quattrocchi,*
                    President/Co-Founder,
                    Workout Anytime Franchising
                    Systems

"Dean Lindsay was phenomenal! Our team left feeling excited and motivated!"   — *Mike Culpepper,*
                    President/COO,
                    1st Heritage Credit, LLC

"Dean Lindsay killed it!!! The best we have ever had."
                    — *Scott Perlmutter,*
                    Director of Operations,
                    Atlantic Hotels Group

"Dean's kickoff was full of energy and inspiration! Our attendees are still reciting some of the quotes weeks later! Thanks for a great keynote, Dean!"
                    — *Katherine Meariman,*
                    VP of Training & Education,
                    Smoothie King Franchises

"Dean message was timely, energizing and funny but most importantly right on point."
                    — *Doug Oathout,*
                    Senior VP, Black Box Corporation

"Our company hired a keynote speaker but got a life-long business partner and resource for our team!"
                    — *David Webster, CEO,*
                    Electrical Components International

For Booking Information, please visit: DeanLindsay.com

Praise for Dean Lindsay's book

How to Achieve Big PHAT Goals

Recommended as one of the
'21 BEST GOAL SETTING BOOKS TO READ'
on PositivePsychology.com.

"Big PHAT Goals is an extremely helpful book for achieving your personal and professional goals."
— Frank Shankwitz, The Creator and
A Founder of the Make-A-Wish Foundation

"I love, love, love this book! As someone who has been dedicated to setting and achieving personal and team goals for the past 30 years, Big PHAT Goals took my understanding to the next level. I rewrote my goals within days of reading the book, following Dean's formula, and I am already experiencing even greater progress! This is a must read for you, as well as those you lead… and those you love!"
— Catherine Monson, CEO,
FASTSIGNS International, Inc.

"… all the best parts of goal achievement knowledge is collated into one powerful little book. … The lessons are scale able, practical and edgy. This is a must have addition for every bookshelf."
— Everyday Manager.com

Connect with Dean Lindsay
on Social Media:

Twitter: **@DeanLindsay**

LinkedIn: **@Dean Lindsay**

Instagram: **@DeanoLindsay**

YouTube Channel: **DeanLindsay**

Facebook: **@DeanLindsayProgressAgent**

Email Dean Lindsay at:

Dean@DeanLindsay.com

Visit

DeanLindsay.com
or call
214-457-5656
for more information.

Dean Lindsay's Customizable Keynote, Workshops & Coaching Programs are designed to Help Empower Progress in Sales, Service and Workplace Culture. *They include:*

Committing to Progress Leadership®:
Say NO to Change Management

Celebrating Service Excellence:
Featuring ForWORDs & BackWORDS:
Words & Phrases That MOVE Business Communication

Rock the Customer Experience:
Featuring the CARE Model

How to Achieve Big PHAT Goals®:
Sales Goals, Team Goals Safety Goals, etc.

Creating Progress in World of Change

Keys to Becoming a Progress Agent®!

Optimism is an Asset:
Keys to Optimizing Your Optimism

Priceless Prospecting®:
Mastering the Lost Art of Business Networking!!

Please visit: **DeanLindsay.com** for more information.

Be Progress.